Management Skills in Schools

Dr Jeff Jones has been a Senior Consultant and Head of Training and Consultancy Unit at CfBT in Reading since 1998. He is an accredited NPQH tutor for the NCSL and has been a team member of the DfES Performance Management initiative as well as being an OFSTED trainer. He is the author of *Monitoring and Evaluation for School Improvement* (2000) and *Performance Management for School Improvement* (2001).

Management Skills in Schools

Dr Jeff Jones

Los Angeles | London | New Delhi
Singapore | Washington DC

First published 2004
Reprinted 2008, 2010, 2011

SAGE Publications Ltd
1 Oliver's Yard
55 City Road
London EC1Y 1SP

SAGE Publications Inc.
2455 Teller Road
Thousand Oaks, California 91320

SAGE Publications India Pvt Ltd
B 1/I 1, Mohan Cooperative Industrial Area
Mathura Road
New Delhi 110 044

SAGE Publications Asia-Pacific Pte Ltd
33 Pekin Street #02-01
Far East Square
Singapore 048763

Library of Congress Control Number: 2003099479

A catalogue record for this book is available from the British Library

ISBN 978 1 4129 0109 3
ISBN 978 1 4129 0110 9 (pbk)

Typeset by TW Typesetting, Plymouth, Devon
Printed in Great Britain by the MPG Books Group

Contents

Introduction

I wanna be the leader
I wanna be the leader
Can I be the leader?
Can I? I can?
Promise? Promise?
Yippee. I'm the leader
I'm the leader

OK, what shall we do?

This book has been written at a time when the direct impact of leadership on the success of schools is increasingly widely accepted. The remit and development agenda of the National College for School Leadership; the growing emphasis being placed by OFSTED in its new framework upon the pivotal part played by effective leadership; and the creation of a team of people to assume strategic leadership roles within the school, are just some of the important initiatives that acknowledge the connection between leadership and successful or improving schools.

Team leadership has always been important in schools, whether at the level of the department, the curriculum area, the key stage, the phase, or in relation to pastoral and leadership teams. This role has assumed even greater significance in the UK in recent years because of the introduction of the mandatory performance management arrangements. In whichever context, team leaders are required to provide professional leadership and management to secure high quality teaching, effective use of resources and improved standards of learning and achievements for all pupils.

The skills required to be an effective team leader in schools are many and varied, but personal management skills lie at the heart of getting the best from those that make up the team. This book is about how team leaders can contribute to overall school improvement and is intended to be a resource for those who lead and manage teams – at all levels – within schools. It focuses on the key personal management skills that each of us needs to develop if we are to support colleagues in the most effective way.

The first chapter looks at what it means to be a highly effective team leader in schools. It helps the reader understand how people become highly effective team leaders; the constraints, demands and choices associated with the role; and, through a series of self-review activities, helps them to gauge their personal effectiveness and competence as team leaders.

Chapter 2 focuses on team leadership and development and acknowledges that although definitions of leadership abound, they have in common a basic belief that leadership is a creative and interpersonal activity that focuses on initiating, enabling and sustaining improvement. The chapter considers ways in which team leaders can challenge the way things happen, their method of working and how they can inspire team members with a clear vision of the way things could or should be. Furthermore, it demonstrates how team leaders can build a collaborative team ethos.

Chapter 3 considers how team leaders, through personal engagement with team members, can model the way forward and motivate team members to achieve beyond what they thought was possible. The chapter describes ways in which team leaders can best put motivational theories into practice and create and sustain a positive working environment.

One of the critical factors in leadership and management success is to control our use of time and priorities. Chapter 4 focuses on strategies and techniques for achieving greater control over these aspects.

For those who have some scope for delegating, Chapter 5 provides helpful guidance for team leaders on the factors that determine effective delegation, together with practical considerations for making delegation worthwhile from the viewpoint of all concerned.

Meetings are likely to continue to be a significant feature of the role of team leaders. Chapter 6 looks at ways of managing meetings more effectively and provides guidance for planning, conducting and evaluating them.

Chapter 7 encourages team leaders to view conflict as an inevitable part of working life. It can occur between team members or between team leaders and staff. Whatever its form, conflict needs to be handled with care and confidence. The chapter looks at the underlying causes of conflict and offers a range of strategies to tackle it – as well as to prevent it happening in the first place.

The focus of Chapter 8 is on taking and implementing decisions. Accomplishing these things consistently well is no mean task and the chapter looks at the constituent skills required of team leaders in their efforts to practise more effective decision-making.

With the introduction of the statutory arrangements for performance management, Chapter 9 provides guidance on preparing for and conducting effective performance reviews. This chapter focuses on how to evaluate performance on an ongoing basis, set realistic performance objectives, and conduct effective performance reviews.

Chapter 10 explores the potential of coaching as a skill for supporting team members in their acquisition of additional skills and knowledge. Central to the coaching relationship is the high quality of personal and interpersonal skills and the development of mutual trust, confidence and respect. The chapter looks not only at a range of factors that will determine the coaching style adopted by team leaders, but also at the consequences of selecting particular styles.

The theme of Chapter 11 is action research. Action research represents a growing field of educational research, the chief identifying feature of which is that it can empower all those involved in the teaching and learning process with the means to improve their practices. This chapter establishes the fundamental principles of action research so that team leaders can grow a culture of professional enquiry within the team. It also provides you with guidance on how to design your own action research project to suit you own aims and professional context.

STRUCTURE OF THE BOOK

This book is intended for those aspiring to, or currently occupying, team leader positions in schools. It acknowledges that team leaders operate at a series of different levels in schools and consequently has been written with the following target audience in mind:

Newly-appointed team leaders

For newly-appointed team leaders, e.g. heads of department, subject/key stage coordinators, the book provides clear and practical guidance to assist you in becoming effective and confident in the role. It will provide advice on key aspects of leadership and management facing you in your new role.

Aspiring team leaders

The book will be of value to aspirants to team leadership because it will introduce you to the concepts, issues and situations that you are likely to face. It will also provide you with knowledge and insights that you may well find form the basis of questions posed at selection interviews for team leader positions.

Existing team leaders

Highly effective team leaders remain constantly open to new ways of improving their personal management skills and reviewing their performance. The book uses a series of self-reflection activities and summaries to help those occupying team leader roles to review the success of their practice and plan for further development.

Each chapter has the following features:

- A brief introduction to the topic under consideration.
- A summary of the key questions that the chapter attempts to address.
- Helpful practical guidance and information presented in a coherent way using accessible language.
- Points for reflection – inviting the reader to consider and pursue points made in the text and to relate the issues and the guidance to their own particular experiences and professional contexts.
- A self-review exercise at the end that encourages the reader to review their professional practice.

1 Being and Becoming a Highly Effective Team Leader

Only those who have fully found themselves in this world can realise their natures. Only those who realise their natures can lead other natures to self-realization. Only those who lead other natures to self-realisation can realize the nature of things.
(Tzu-Ssu, a grandson of Confucius)

INTRODUCTION

Tzu-Ssu's wise words about self-knowledge and self-realization may seem a little divorced from the reality of school life when you are trying to deal with next year's timetable; deficit budgets; yet more changes to the syllabus; boys' underperformance; and the underperformance of a colleague. Yet, at the heart of this chapter, and indeed the book, is the need for each of us as team leaders to understand the intimate relationship between knowing, understanding and developing ourselves and knowing, understanding and developing our team members. This chapter provides guidance to aspiring and existing team leaders by responding to the following questions:

➢ What is the key to effective team leadership?

➢ How do I become a highly effective team leader?

➢ What about the constraints, demands and choices associated with my team leadership role?

➢ What are the characteristics of highly effective leaders?

➢ How can I gauge my personal effectiveness as a team leader?

➢ How can I gauge my competence as a team leader?

➢ What is meant by leadership style? How important is this in leading a team?

➢ How can I help to improve the quality of what we do and achieve as a team?

WHAT IS THE KEY TO EFFECTIVE TEAM LEADERSHIP?

Effective team leadership relies upon mastering a wide assortment of skills; skills ranging from implementing policies and organizing procedures to motivating staff to achieve high standards. The aim of team leadership is to assist members of the team to achieve their personal best. To achieve this, team leaders have to:

- set high, but realistic, performance objectives, not only for themselves, but also for team colleagues;

- find ways to improve existing practices and policies; and

- meet and, better still, exceed current standards of learning, teaching, and pupil achievement.

It is this latter point that provides the focus and rationale for the team leader's role. However, before team leaders and their teams can achieve their goals, it is important that they are clear about expectations relating to how things might be done and the standards of performance that need to be reached, for example, through the school's improvement plan. Communicating these expectations to others is an important next step. In this way, team leaders can also demonstrate their commitment to the key task of improving quality. Maintaining and improving existing standards is, of course, an ongoing process that requires team leaders to impress upon their team the importance of analysing the problem areas they encounter and of working together to find solutions. Involving staff in this way helps not only to generate fresh ideas but also to create a climate of participation and increased motivation.

Point for reflection
How do you currently involve your team in looking for ways to improve standards, practices, processes and performance? Which methods have you found to be most successful?

HOW DO I BECOME A HIGHLY EFFECTIVE TEAM LEADER?

Highly effective leadership, particularly in the role of team leader, is of crucial importance to the success of any school. How you perform now, and how you might perform in the future, often depends on career experiences and on opportunities for reflecting on these experiences. How you are perceived as a team leader will affect the attitude and performance of those both 'above' and 'below' you. Because team leaders do not work in isolation, they have to display a complex mix of different styles, qualities and attitudes to be effective. These important skills and qualities are likely to derive from your perceptions of the effectiveness of team leaders that you have worked with and the values that underpin your approach.

Point for reflection
Think of a team leader you know who, in your view, is ineffective in the role. Suggest reasons why she or he fails to provide adequate leadership. Now, think of a team leader who you consider is effective. Why do you consider him or her to be successful?

To be highly effective as team leaders we need to know something about ourselves. In doing so, we expand the range of behaviours upon which we can

Table 1.1 **A model of management competence (based on Boydell, 1985)**

Level	Characteristics
Level one – Manager as technician	• focuses on performing standard routines and procedures • places great store on responding to things correctly
Level two – Manager as professional	• develops a personal style of doing things • accumulates personal knowledge • builds systems of knowledge rather than collections of unrelated facts • synthesizes ideas • chooses effectively from alternative courses of action • does not rely on standard, correct, pre-determined solutions • monitors own decisions • develops increasing levels of self-awareness • learns consciously from experience • makes personal sense out of what is happening • generates creative ideas • looks at old problems in a new way
Level three – Manager as artist	• fully understands what it means to be a manager/leader • understands and displays personal standards and values • fully understands how the work fits with all other aspects of personal and professional life

draw in different situations. Several models exist that help us to understand our own development. For example, Boydell (1985) proposes a model of management competence that has three levels (Table 1.1).

The usefulness of Boydell's model in helping you analyse the development you are now undertaking as a leader, is that it provides a perception of where you might be heading so that ultimately you have a fuller insight of what it means to you personally to be a highly effective team leader. This self-development is the product of making sense of your own experiences and dealing with challenges as they impinge upon your professional and personal life. In effect, self-development is about change *of* self, *by* self (Figure 1.1) – itself a form of learning. Pedler, Burgoyne and Boydell (1986) refer to this as 'managing ME':

> Managing ME is the first step for the self-developer – unless I take charge of myself, how can I take charge of situations; unless I create order in myself how can I contribute to creating order with others? Managing ME first is the key of self-empowerment and the empowerment of others.

Leaders and managers who are comfortable operating at a technician level, focusing on routine administrative tasks, often lack the confidence to deal with outcomes that are unpredictable or vague. A major dimension of effective leadership is having enough confidence in yourself and in your ability to respond appropriately in given circumstances. Ultimately, of course, this entails knowing yourself, your strengths and weaknesses and learning from the everyday experiences presented to you in the role. For Boydell (1985), self-development involves personal change:

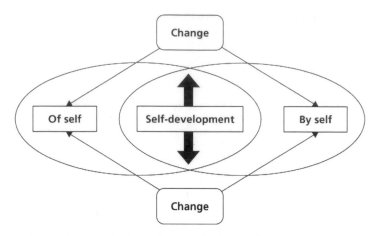

Figure 1.1 Self-development is about change of self by self

it is not just about improving, refining and adding to what you have already, but about moving out of comfort zones, expanding your personal limits and aiming for peak performance. It involves changes in thinking, feeling and willing . . .

Point for reflection

Having considered Boydell's three-level model of competence, where would you locate your existing competence level as a leader and manager? Which areas lend themselves to further improvement? What development opportunities might be most helpful for you to seek to bring about these improvements?

WHAT ABOUT THE CONSTRAINTS, DEMANDS AND CHOICES ASSOCIATED WITH MY TEAM LEADERSHIP ROLE?

Anyone with leadership and management responsibilities in schools is faced with choices, demands and constraints in relation to their role. Performing a role as important as team leader is dependent on a set of separate, but interacting, influences:

- personal characteristics, e.g. personality, skills, motivation;

- self-presentation, e.g. visibility, profile, role modelling;

- self-organization, e.g. time management, stress management, selecting priorities;

- self-development, e.g. reflection, career aspirations, development opportunities; and

- situational characteristics, e.g. school context, team maturity, length of experience.

Point for reflection

This is an opportunity for you to analyse your own performance as a team leader in the light of the constraints, demands and choices associated with your leadership role.

- Identify *constraints* on you in your team leadership role (they may derive from resource considerations; national, local or school policy; people's attitudes; time; etc.).
- Identify *demands* on you as a team leader (they may derive from national, local or school policies; the extent and nature of your responsibilities; the types of relationship you have with colleagues; etc.).
- Now list some *choices* you make in:
  - *how* you do your work
  - *what* work you do
  - *how* you work with others

It will come as no surprise to anyone that managing a diversity of roles brings significant pressures and challenges. In performing their roles, team leaders may experience some or all of the role strains examined in Table 1.2.

Point for reflection

Taking into account the nature and extent of your role, identify examples of the different kinds of 'role strain' that you may have experienced or are currently experiencing. In what ways are the four concepts identified in Table 1.2 useful for understanding others' behaviours, as well your own.

Table 1.2 Team leaders' experiences of their role

Role	Experience
Role ambiguity	In this situation, team leaders believe that there is insufficient information available describing their role. The result is a lack of clarity about the precise nature of the role, e.g. the parameters of the role are ill-defined leading to duplication of effort or important functions not being carried out.
Role conflict	Here, the team leader may be uncomfortable with particular role requirements, e.g. a pastoral team leader whose views on school uniform are quite relaxed having to enforce the school's rule that students should be in uniform on school trips.
Role overload	Team leaders, in these circumstances, feel unable to fulfil the range of expected roles because of sheer work overload. Team leaders are often required to take on additional tasks brought on by, say, increased legislation but find that few if any tasks are removed to make way for them.
Role underload	This occurs when team leaders' expectations of the role exceed those of the organization, e.g. assistant team leaders being given routine administrative tasks.

WHAT ARE THE CHARACTERISTICS OF HIGHLY EFFECTIVE TEAM LEADERS?

A trawl through the literature suggests that there are certain attitudes, key behaviours, leadership styles and management approaches that appear to characterize the more effective team leaders. Among them are the following:

- Strategic leaders are able to picture a range of possibilities several stages ahead of the current phase of organizational development. It was said of Napoleon that like a good chess player he could envisage several steps ahead and consider various permutations.

- Strategic leadership is pragmatic rather than 'head in the clouds'. The strategies developed will lead to tactics which will need to engage with and succeed in the real school world. These strategies must therefore be based on a realistic appraisal of the environment in which the school finds itself, the resources at its disposal and the opportunities that exist.

- Strategic leaders have a great sense of timing – they have the patience to wait until the time is right to make a major intervention, yet have the boldness to strike decisively when the moment is right. They and their schools are alert and ready to seize an opportunity.

- Leaders whose current work is future-focused are more likely to be working strategically. They invest their time in developing people and their capability for the future of the school, as well as managing the current needs of the school.

- A strategic leader is willing to work with others in alliances and agreements to make a more significant intervention than either party would be able to make alone. If necessary, the strategic leader is willing to subordinate the school's need for recognition to making progress against a broader agenda for change.

Point for reflection

Review the above characteristics of highly effective strategic leaders. To what extent do you display these characteristics? Who in your team is able to contribute to strategic considerations and discussions in a meaningful way?

HOW CAN I GAUGE MY PERSONAL EFFECTIVENESS AS A TEAM LEADER?

To be effective, your team leadership behaviour needs to be consciously directed and controlled. This implies a need to understand yourself and your actions. In her book, *The Successful Self* (1989), the psychotherapist, Dorothy Rowe describes the successful or effective person as having:

- *Awareness* – not only an insight into themselves but also into others;

- *Understanding* – holding theories about the causes of events and people's behaviour, but also being aware of how these theories are formed.

She goes on to suggest six characteristics of a successful self, which complement these core elements of awareness and understanding:

- feeling valuable, self-accepting and self-confident;

- not engaged in a constant battle to preserve their personal reputation;

- flexible and creative in developing themselves in ways that are congruent with their sense of who they are and their purpose in life;

- using their view of the world as a basis for making their own decisions and being creative;

- having developed the skills to understand and work with other views of the world; and

- having created a life story for themselves that gives a sense of progress – past events are interpreted in a positive light and are seen as leading to a positive future.

On the same theme, Covey, in *The Seven Habits of Highly Effective People* (1989), proposed that the concept of personal effectiveness is, in fact, based on 'character' which he describes as:

> creating an empowering center of correct maps from which an individual can effectively solve problems, maximize opportunities and continually learn and integrate other principles in an upward spiral of growth.

He believes that our character is a composite of our habits because 'they are consistent, often unconscious patterns; they constantly, daily, express our character and produce our effectiveness ... or ineffectiveness'. His seven habits of highly effective people which form the basis of character are shown in Table 1.3.

Table 1.3 **The seven habits of highly effective people**

Habit	Characteristics
Independence	1. Be proactive 2. Do things with an end in mind 3. Manage your personal priorities
Interdependence	4. Operate on a win-win basis 5. Empathize – first understand, then be understood 6. Work to create synergy
Renewal	7. Preserve and enhance your productive capacity – physical, socio/emotional, mental and spiritual

Point for reflection

In his book, *The Seven Habits of Highly Effective People*, Stephen Covey maintains that habits have tremendous 'gravity pull', which we may need to break out of if we are to enhance our effectiveness. Breaking these 'deeply embedded habitual tendencies such as procrastination, impatience, criticalness or selfishness that violate basic principles of human effectiveness involves more than a little will-power'. Think for a moment about your, and your team's, 'habitual tendencies'. How might the more desirable tendencies be strengthened and the non-desirable ones eradicated or their effect minimized?

HOW CAN I GAUGE MY COMPETENCE AS A TEAM LEADER?

At this point in your reading, you may find it useful to spend a little time in gauging your own capabilities in whatever team leadership role you currently occupy. For example, you may be head of a primary school, a subject coordinator for maths and technology, pastoral head of the upper section of a high school, a Special Education Needs Coordinator (SENCO), or assistant headteacher within the schools' leadership group. However, it may be that you are aspiring to one of those positions, in which case the exercise is just as valuable because it provides you with a professional development agenda. Whatever your particular role and perspective, come to a personal view about your existing competences by working through Table 1.4. You do not score this exercise but the nearer your level of competence is to the descriptors set out in column D, the more advanced is your development in relation to that competency. There are at least three ways in which you can complete this exercise to gain valuable insights into your present level of effectiveness:

1. Consider each of the competences in turn and, from the four descriptors, select the one that most accurately describes the current situation. This is a useful exercise and may offer you a view of how well advanced your skills are in particular areas. As important is the perspective this exercise offers you on what you might need to attend to in order to develop new or more advanced skills. This can be useful when discussing your development objectives and opportunities with your own team leader in the performance management review.

2. Complete the exercise as described above, but share your perceptions with one or more colleagues who know what your role entails and the way you perform it. Use this as an opportunity to gain constructive feedback, using actual examples, of the way you currently do things and how you might improve on the way in which you do things in the future. This could be a useful part of your performance management review.

3. Again, complete the exercise as described in (1) above and try to identify some concrete evidence to support your views, e.g. things that people have said, actions that have resulted in improvements. In short, when you have

Table 1.4 Gauging your competences as a team leader

Competences		Descriptors		
	A	B	C	D
How competent am I at developing and motivating my team?	• My team members know what is expected of them individually and collectively.	• My team members understand each other's roles and work together to reach their goals.	• My team members are enthusiastic about team goals, their part of the whole, and engage in activities that ensure team and individuals succeed.	• My team members develop and 'own' the team's priorities and goals.
How competent am I at facilitating team discussion and problem-solving processes?	• I lead discussion without forcing my personal position. • I am an active participant in discussion. • I work through a set agenda in a logical and planned way.	• I elicit contributions from all team members in discussion.	• I enable the team to reach a decision by posing questions and probing. • I support team member contributions.	• I respond to the needs of the team while enabling them to move forward. • I recognize and deal with barriers to progress.
How competent am I at recognizing and managing diverse opinions and working styles?	• I recognize differences but limit or discourage different opinions.	• I encourage individuals to express different views but limit extensive discussion and seek to maintain the norm.	• I seek different opinions and guide the team in maximizing the benefits of the differences.	• I enable others to recognize the value of diversity. • I encourage team members to seek alternative perspectives and use the information to generate new ideas.
How competent am I to understand and work with different learning styles?	• I recognize my own learning style.	• I recognize different learning styles in others and attempt to accommodate.	• I help the team identify different learning styles and respect their preferences.	• I enable the team to assess, understand and maximize different learning styles to achieve improved outcomes.

Table 1.4 Continued

Competences	A	B	C	D
			Descriptors	
How competent am I at establishing and maintaining rapport with individual team members?	• I recognize different communication and personality styles.	• I understand the different approaches required for different members of the team. • I am flexible and adaptable in responding to the needs of the team.	• I use and adapt communication approaches for each member of the team. • I confidently deal with individuals and issues as they arise. • I think well on my feet.	• I adjust style and approach in different situations to accommodate communication needs of individuals. • I am viewed as credible, self-confident and genuinely interested in enabling the success of the team.
How competent am I at resolving conflict?	• I sometimes leave disagreement unaddressed. • I hope that conflict will resolve itself or diminish over time.	• I address and resolve disagreement but not always to the satisfaction of each party.	• I confront conflict in a non-judgemental way and build on understanding of different frames of reference, to push towards agreement.	• I am capable of using conflict to produce new, creative win-win solutions and opportunities.
How competent am I at displaying listening skills?	• I listen to what people say and use their ideas if they match my views.	• I take notes, feed back items and issues to the team. I make and communicate decisions to ensure common understanding.	• I accurately integrate and build on comments and ideas. • I value high levels of contribution from the team.	• I make the team feel at ease and give complete attention during discussion. • My body language and verbal cues show that I am internalizing what is being said.
How competent am I at facilitating shared responsibility and providing	• I lead discussions, meetings and decision-making.	• I enable the team to share agenda and priority setting.	• I enable consensus-style decision-making to occur.	• I encourage dynamic interaction which drives direction and priorities.

team leadership?	• I do not encourage team members to act or position themselves to contribute on an equal basis.	• I encourage the team to brainstorm and assist in decision-making. • I provide information to develop the team's level of knowledge.	• I identify context and parameters around which the team can resolve issues.	• I recognize and use individual expertise. • I encourage the team to challenge ideas and generate others.
How competent am I at solving problems?	• I react to situations. • I like 'fire-fighting' with short-term solutions.	• I support others in identifying problems and potential solutions.	• I identify and teach others to recognize the warning signs of problems in the making.	• I lead a systematic analysis of problems and generate creative solutions. • I have contingency plans in place to assist in solving problems.
How competent am I to deal with complex and multiple ideas?	• I focus primarily on one idea or concept at a time. • I am uncomfortable with interruptions, changes to task, or requests to handle additional tasks at the same time.	• I can handle several tasks, projects and responsibilities at once. Unexpected changes may result in digression.	• I am able to think in diverse ways and incorporate changes that are required.	• I can 'multi-task' and see cause and effect relationships. • I am aware of the ramifications of change to one part of the system and plan for it.
How competent am I at maintaining personal energy and dynamism?	• I am focused and energetic for brief periods of time during discussions.	• I remain focused and demonstrate energy for the entire discussion.	• I am able to focus and expend considerable concentration over protracted periods of time as required.	• I consistently convey high energy and focused attention in all interactions.
How competent am I at stimulating and supporting creativity and innovation in others?	• I am aware of creativity and innovation in the team's practice.	• I encourage new thinking, reward success and good attempts. • I encourage individuals to take initiative.	• I lead by example. • I encourage creativity and innovation within the team. • I help team members evaluate and strengthen their own ideas.	• I create an environment where creativity and innovation are seen as a source of strategic advantage and are rewarded.

selected a descriptor that best summarizes your personal perception, simply ask: 'How do I know?' 'Where is the evidence that shows that?' This can result in a very comprehensive self review in preparation for your performance management review.

WHAT IS MEANT BY LEADERSHIP STYLE? HOW IMPORTANT IS THIS IN LEADING A TEAM?

Your leadership style is the pattern of behaviour that you adopt with your team, to plan, organize, motivate and control its activities and performance. It is the extent and manner in which you listen, set goals and performance standards, develop and implement action plans, guide and direct others, provide feedback, etc. Research over many years, (e.g. Tannenbaum and Schmidt, 1959; Blake and Mouton, 1964; White and Lippitt, 1983; Leithwood, Jantzi and Steinbach, 1999; Gunter, 2001) has shown that leadership styles are important because of their impact on how individuals within a team feel, and the extent to which they are motivated to perform at higher levels and therefore have a greater impact on standards. Highly effective team leaders use a range of leadership styles to suit the requirements of the various situations they encounter. By doing so they create a context and a climate in which staff will want to succeed at the core purpose – securing higher standards of pupil achievement.

It is not the intention here to describe all existing leadership models and styles. This section simply identifies six leadership styles that you can consider and so form a view of their relevance, or otherwise, to your professional context. Table 1.5 sets out these styles and describes the circumstances in which they are most and least effective.

Point for reflection

Having considered the six styles of leadership outlined in Table 1.5, what views have you come to about their relative strengths and deficiencies? Which style do you favour and why? Is there a mismatch between the style you favour, the one you employ most regularly, and the one that your team respond to best?

HOW CAN I HELP TO IMPROVE THE QUALITY OF WHAT WE DO AND ACHIEVE AS A TEAM?

In their efforts to improve the quality of what they and their team do, one of the first tasks for team leaders is to define key standards: standards that are so crucial that they stand apart from others because of their potential to impact directly on learning, teaching and pupil achievement. These key standards, and methods for achieving them, are described in Table 1.6.

The Teachers' Standards Framework (DfES, 2001a) is helpful for supporting team leaders at all levels within schools – subject leaders, SENCOs, Advanced Skills Teachers and headteachers – because it sets out the expectations for

Table 1.5 Six styles of leadership

Leadership style	What does the leader do?	When is it most effective?	When is it least effective?
Coercive	• provides directives • does not listen or encourage much staff input • expects staff compliance • controls tightly using close monitoring • relies on negative, corrective feedback • motivates by pointing out negative consequences of poor performance	• when applied to relatively clear-cut tasks • in crisis situations, when the leader has more information than staff • when the failure of staff to comply leads to serious consequences • with underperformers who have not been able to respond to support e.g. coaching	• when applied to complex tasks • over an extended period of time – staff are not being developed • with skilled and self-motivated staff capable of directing and monitoring their own work
Authoritative	• takes responsibility for developing and relaying a clear direction • invites perspective of others to plan the way forward • explains the vision at every opportunity • sets standards and monitors performance • enhances motivation using balanced positive and negative feedback	• when a new vision or direction is needed • when tasks are routine and staff performance adequate • when the leader is perceived to be the expert or authority • with staff who rely on their leader for guidance	• when the leader lacks professional credibility • when the staff have greater expertise than the leader • when trying to promote self-managing teams or participatory decision-making
Affiliative	• focuses on promoting friendly interactions among staff • places more emphasis on meeting staff • places more emphasis on meeting staff's emotional needs than on defining goals, tasks and standards	• when used in conjunction with others styles • when giving personal support • in getting diverse groups of people to work together harmoniously	• when staff performance is inadequate and corrective feedback on performance is necessary for improvement • in crises or complex situations needing clear direction and control

Table 1.5 Continued

Leadership style	What does the leader do?	When is it most effective?	When is it least effective?
Affiliative	• pays attention to and cares for the whole person and stresses things that keep people happy • identifies opportunities for positive feedback and avoid performance-related confrontations • rewards personal characteristics sometimes as much as job performance		• with members of staff who are task-oriented or less concerned about forming friendships with their team leader
Democratic	• trusts that staff have the skills to develop the right direction for themselves and the school • invites staff to take decisions affecting their work • reaches decisions through consensus • uses regular meetings to listen to staff concerns • rewards adequate performance and rarely gives negative feedback	• when staff are competent and as well informed and knowledgeable as the team leader • when staff need coordination • when the team leader is unclear about the best approach or direction and has staff with clearer ideas • after using the authoritative style to champion the vision, this style will provide the support and guidance needed	• in crises, when there is no time to hold meetings • when staff lack competence, crucial information or need close supervision
Pacesetting	• leads by example or by modelling desired outcomes and behaviour • displays high standards and expects others to know the rationale behind what is being modelled		

Style			
	• delegates tasks only to those who have his or her confidence that they will be carried out to high standards • removes responsibility for tasks if high performance is not imminent • shows little sympathy for poor performance • rescues situations or gives detailed task instructions if staff experience difficulties	• when staff need little direction due to their high motivation and competence • when quick results are required • for developing staff who resemble the team leader	• when the team leader cannot do all the work personally • when staff need direction, development and coordination
Coaching	• helps staff to identify their strengths and weaknesses in the light of their goals and aspirations • encourages staff to establish development goals • seeks agreement with staff on their respective roles in the development process • provides ongoing advice and feedback	• when staff acknowledge a discrepancy between their current and desired levels of performance • with staff who are motivated to take initiative, innovative and are enthusiastic about developing professionally	• when the leader lacks credibility • when staff require much direction and feedback • in crisis situations

Table 1.6 Improving standards of quality

Key standards	Approaches to securing these key standards
Leadership – leading the team towards high performance by seeking continuous improvement in all that they do.	Ensure that team members are focused on continuous improvement of all aspects of their performance. Recognize and acknowledge individuals within the team for the success of their efforts
Strategy – developing the team vision, values and strategic direction	Establish all objectives with the aim of reaching the highest quality standards. Communicate and reinforce aims clearly to all, and review and update them regularly
Staff – ensuring that team members are motivated, well managed and empowered to develop and improve	Develop all team members in the skills and competences they need to meet their improvement objectives. Communicate in ways that are appropriate for individuals as well as the whole team using a range of media
Resources – using financial and other resources efficiently to achieve key objectives	Ensure finances are managed efficiently and everyone knows what is happening and why. Invest in the most appropriate technology to support team members in managing their time and priorities
Processes – ensuring that all policies and processes are consistently highly effective	Agree performance measures and provide feedback to maintain the momentum for improvement. Encourage team colleagues to formulate innovative ideas for improving practices and processes

effective performance in different roles. It maps the standards that currently exist, and the expectations they contain. It shows how the expectations of teachers can grow and change at different stages of a career as they assume different roles within schools. It helps them to recognize their existing expertise and achievements as well as any development needs they may have. The framework summarizes the key elements in each of the standards under ten dimensions of teaching and leadership within a school:

- knowledge and understanding;
- planning and setting expectations;
- teaching and managing pupil learning;
- assessment and evaluation;
- pupil achievement;
- relations with parents and the wider community;
- maaging own performance and development;
- managing and developing staff and other adults;
- managing resources;
- strategic leadership.

Point for reflection

Table 1.7, which is adapted from *The Teachers' Standards Framework*, sets out the standards that (i) subject leaders, and (ii) headteachers would be expected to achieve within the strategic leadership dimension. Select one of these roles and comment on the value of the standards framework in helping you gauge your existing personal effectiveness and professional competence, as well as your development needs.

Table 1.7 Standards framework for subject leaders and headteachers (adapted from DfES, 2001a)

Role	Strategic leadership
Subject leaders	• Create a climate which enables other staff to develop and maintain positive attitudes towards the subject and confidence in teaching it. • Develop and implement policies and practices for the subject which reflect the school's commitment to high achievement, effective teaching and learning. • Ensure that the headteacher, senior managers and governors are well informed about subject policies, plans and priorities, the success in meeting objectives and targets, and subject-related professional development plans. • Establish a clear, shared understanding of the importance and role of the subject in contributing to pupils' spiritual, moral, cultural, mental and physical development, and in preparing pupils for the opportunities, responsibilities and experiences of adult life.
Headteachers	• Create an ethos and provide educational vision and direction which secure effective teaching, successful learning and achievement by pupils and sustained improvement in their spiritual, moral, cultural, mental and physical development, and prepare them for the opportunities, responsibilities and experiences of adult life; and secure the commitment to the vision and direction of the school. • Present a coherent and accurate account of the school's performance in a form appropriate to a range of audiences, including governors, the LEA, the local community, OFSTED and others, to enable them to play their part effectively. • Lead by example, provide inspiration and motivation, and embody for the pupils, staff, governors and parents vision, purpose and the leadership of the school. • Ensure that all those involved in the school are committed to its aims and are accountable in meeting long-, medium- and short-term objectives to secure school improvement, and targets which secure the educational success of the school. • Ensure that the management, finance, organization and administration of the school support its vision and aims. • Provide information, objective advice and support to the governing body to enable it to meet its responsibilities for securing effective teaching and learning and improved standards of achievements, and for achieving efficiency and value for money.

SUMMARY SELF-REVIEW

Spend a little time considering and then responding to the following review questions:

1. How readily do I ignore small mistakes made by team members and focus on more important matters?

2. How well do I accept criticism from others?

3. How relaxed am I when dealing with others at work?

4. How secure and confident am I in my role?

5. How readily do I give credit to the team for high standards of achievement?

6. How fair and just am I in my dealings with others?

7. In what ways do I convey feelings of security to the team?

8. In what ways do I convey a sense of friendliness and concern for the problems of others?

9. In what ways do I show respect for the people I work with?

10. How well do I communicate and motivate my team?

11. How would I gauge the quality of my participation in helping the team achieve its goals?

12. What evidence do I have that the team respects me?

13. How readily do I accept the opinions of others, even when they differ from my own?

14. How effective am I in keeping the team together at times of crisis?

15. Faced with a choice between speed and perfection, which one am I likely to choose?

16. How effective am I at distinguishing between things that are urgent and things that are important?

17. How effective am I at promoting the creativity and innovation skills of my team?

18. On what basis do I believe that I perform tasks well?

19. In what ways do I communicate the standards that I expect?

20. What evidence do I have that my leadership style is appropriate?

Action planning

Having spent some time reviewing your approach to being and becoming an effective team leader, identify some actions that you might take to strengthen your current approach.

2 Leading and Developing Teams

It is the responsibility of the leadership and the management to give opportunities and put demands on people which enable them to grow as human beings in their work environment.

(Sir John Harvey-Jones, former ICI chief)

INTRODUCTION

Working in teams is increasingly being seen as preferred practice in schools and in many other organizations, where traditional hierarchies are giving way to flatter organizational structures, but also in order to develop more effective working practices. Team leadership is about influencing the activities of a team towards achieving team goals. The task of team leaders is not only to achieve goals – school and team – but also to build an effective team and draw the best from each member of the team. By addressing the following questions, this chapter offers practical guidance to team leaders on leading and developing their team:

➢ Why is there so much emphasis on team leadership in schools?

➢ What exactly do we mean by leadership? Is there a distinction between leadership and management?

➢ What is a team? How does it differ from a group?

➢ What is the key purpose of developing teams in schools?

➢ What makes a 'good' team? What does successful teamwork depend upon?

➢ What should I attempt to do to build teamwork?

➢ How can I gauge the quality of the teamwork?

WHY IS THERE SO MUCH EMPHASIS ON TEAM LEADERSHIP IN SCHOOLS?

Team leadership in schools is one of the most difficult attributes to describe. Each of us may have quite different views on whether leadership is a science or an art, whether leaders are born or made, and so on, but it is likely that we would all agree that team leadership in schools should make a positive difference to the lives of young people and the staff who support them. With this in mind, team leadership should be dynamic and about:

- change – by seeking improvement and, if necessary, moving from the status quo;

- promoting new ideas – by encouraging and utilizing the creativity of others;

- gaining better outcomes – by seeking continuous but realistic improvement;

- striving to implement policy – by consistently applying standard operating procedures;

- living a philosophy – by establishing and sharing beliefs and values; and

- fully engaging staff within the school – by maximizing the skills of our most valuable resource.

Effective leadership in schools matters because it has the potential to impact on:

- People – School staff, like other workers, spend most of their lives at work. Whereas this can cause stress, frustration, boredom and conflict, it can also be extremely positive because of the relationships that are built, the opportunities on offer to show ingenuity, creativity and a range of associated skills, as well as to develop, grow and achieve. Team leaders create professional and personal development opportunities;

- Schools and wider society – Organizations, such as schools, are the bedrock of our society. Leadership in schools is about creating a climate and providing opportunities for young people to maximize their full potential. Good leadership gives the '*why*' to what people do in schools.

WHAT EXACTLY DO WE MEAN BY LEADERSHIP? IS THERE A DISTINCTION BETWEEN LEADERSHIP AND MANAGEMENT?

You have only to look on the shelves of a university library or your local bookshop to witness the plethora of books on leadership. Not surprisingly, these authors are proposing their own definitions and interpretations of leadership. The purpose of this chapter is not to provide the definitive definition of leadership – no such thing exists probably – but to offer a small selection of definitions and descriptions, to stimulate thoughts about, and reactions to, the relative emphases contained within each.

Point for reflection

What follows is a small selection of definitions of the term 'leadership'. Consider each and form a view on the comparative strengths of each based on your practical experience of working in schools:

- '*Leadership is a reciprocal relationship between those who choose to lead and those who decide to follow*' (Kouzes and Posner, 1993).

- *'Leadership is the process of influencing the activities of an individual or a group in efforts towards goal achievement in a given situation'* (Hersey and Blanchard, 1977).
- *'All managers are by definition leaders in that they can only do what they have to do with the support of their team, who must be inspired or persuaded to follow them'* (Armstrong, 1994).
- *'We are coming to believe that leaders are those people who "walk ahead", people who are genuinely committed to deep change in themselves and in their organizations. They lead through developing new skills, capabilities, and understandings. And they come from many places within the organization'* (Senge et al., 1996).

The debate continues over the differences between leadership and management. For many, they are interchangeable terms. For others, they represent very distinctive meanings and properties. Law and Glover (2000), helpfully, provide some of the typical distinctions that are drawn between leadership and management in the research literature (see Table 2.1). As our understanding has increased in recent years it is clear that there are not only important differences between the two terms but also significant overlaps.

In practice, however, the distinctions between leadership and management are not clear. School leaders are constantly being required to interchange and integrate their roles. Both are 'integrally and inseparably related' (MacBeath and Myers, 1999). This means that successful leadership and management will rely heavily on the overlapping skills of leadership, management, and administration. The same authors (Law and Glover, 2000)

Table 2.1 Distinctions between leadership and management (based on Law & Glover, 2002)

Management	Leadership
'Building and maintaining an organisational structure' (Schein, 1885)	*'Building and maintaining an organisational culture'* (Schein, 1885)
'Path-following' (Hodgson, 1987)	*'Path-finding'* (Hodgson, 1987)
'Doing things right' (Bennis and Nanus, 1985)	*'Doing the right things'* (Bennis and Nanus, 1985)
'The manager maintains . . . relies on control' (Bennis, 1989)	*'The leader develops . . . inspires trust'* (Bennis, 1989)
'A preoccupation with the here-and-now of goal attainment' (Bryman, 1986)	*'Focused on the creation of a vision about a desired future state'* (Bryman, 1986)
'Managers maintain a low level of emotional involvement' (Zaleznik, 1977)	*'Leaders have empathy with other people and give attention to what events and actions mean'* (Zaleznik, 1977)
'Designing and carrying out plans, getting things done, working effectively with people' (Louis and Miles, 1992)	*'Establishing a mission . . . giving a sense of direction'* (Louis and Miles, 1992)
'Being taught by the organisation' (Hodgson, 1987)	*'Learning from the organisation'* (Hodgson, 1987)

Table 2.2 Leadership, management and administration in schools (based on Law and Glover, 2000)

	Headteacher	Subject leader/ coordinator	Class teacher
Focus	• whole school	• subject department	• curriculum delivery
Through	• school improvement plan	• departmental improvement plan	• schemes of work
Leadership	• vision • aims and objectives • strategy • team formation • school policies	• departmental aims • targets • resource bidding • team cohesion • subject policies	• classroom tone • subject mission • teaching and learning style
Management	• overall control of resource base • over development of staff	• resource allocation • team development • curriculum and organization • monitoring and evaluation • student progress	• materials development • resource use • curriculum tracking • student assessment
Administration	• responsible but not 'hands-on'	• staff records • resource tracking	• student records • teaching and learning records

illustrate this overlapping tendency across various school roles using the outline shown in Table 2.2.

Point for reflection

What distinctions do you draw between leadership, management and administration? How would you describe each in terms of what you do and how you do things in your team leadership role?

WHAT IS A TEAM? HOW DOES IT DIFFER FROM A GROUP?

The terms 'team' and 'group' are often used interchangeably. While 'group' can be a generic term covering two or more people working together, the term 'team' conveys a deliberate assembling of people charged with achieving a task or tasks. It is probably self-evident that teams make a necessary contribution to the success of schools and that schools should encourage and value effective teamwork. However, it is also important that a team has a clear focus on its processes and performance standards. According to Everard and Morris (1996), for example:

> A team is a group of people that can effectively tackle any task which it has been set to do. The contribution drawn from each member is of the highest possible quality, and is one which could not have been called into play other than in the context of a supportive team.

When it comes to the term 'team', there is no shortage of definitions and most of them point out that teams do not perform successfully as teams simply because they are described as teams. High-performing teams need to cooperate and work together on a common task. Another perspective on teamwork is the one provided by Bell (1992) who defined it as a group of people working together on the basis of:

- shared perceptions;
- a common purpose;
- agreed procedures;
- commitment;
- cooperation; and
- resolving disagreements openly by discussion.

It is interesting to think of Bell's definition in the light of the teams we lead or are members of. These days, schools abound with teams of one kind or another. The number and size of these teams often reflects the size and structure of individual schools. In a typical secondary school, for example, it is likely that the teams in place will be those shown in Figure 2.1.

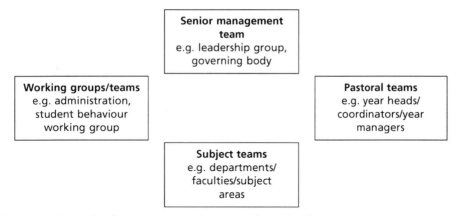

Figure 2.1 **Example of team structures in a secondary school**

Point for reflection

You may want to think about Everard and Morris's earlier definition for a moment and compare it with other definitions you may have come across, not least your own.

WHAT IS THE KEY PURPOSE OF DEVELOPING TEAMS IN SCHOOLS?

According to Woodcock (1979), organizations such as schools benefit from the uniqueness that teams have to offer: 'they can make things happen which would not happen if the team did not exist'. Determining the purpose of the team is critical to effective school leadership. Handy (1993) suggests that teams might undertake the following functions or purposes in organizations such as schools:

- distributing and managing work;
- problem-solving and decision-making;
- enabling people to take part in decision-making;
- coordinating and liaising;
- passing on information;
- negotiating or conflict resolution;
- increasing commitment and involvement; and
- monitoring and evaluating.

Point for reflection
Think of a team you lead and ask yourself how it differs from groups operating in your school. What distinctions have you drawn between group and team?

WHAT MAKES A 'GOOD' TEAM? WHAT DOES SUCCESSFUL TEAMWORK DEPEND UPON?

Earlier definitions remind us that successful teams demonstrate the same consistent and fundamental features. These are:

- strong and purposeful leadership;
- precise goals and objectives;
- informed decision-making;
- decisive action;
- free communication;
- skills and techniques;
- clear targets for team members; and
- balance of team members.

The ability to create a team is generally viewed as one of the most significant attributes of those in leadership positions. There are a number of ways in which team leaders can encourage and produce effective teamwork. Successful teamwork depends on:

- a clearly defined set of aims and objectives;

- the skills and qualities of the person leading the team; and

- the personalities and attributes of team members.

Point for reflection

Think of two or three teams to which you belong. Using the checklist below, which teams do you think are the most and least well developed? In your view, what key factors have contributed to their development? Identify the factors that have hindered their development.

The group is effective at getting things done		The group is ineffective at getting things done
Membership is vague and easy to achieve.		Membership is defined and difficult to achieve.
Group has clear standards of behaviour.		Group has little influence on behaviour of its members.
There is no clear difference of roles.		Individuals have clearly different roles.
There are close personal relationships within the group.		Relationships are mainly Impersonal.
People have a low understanding of group purpose.		People share a clear understanding of group purpose.
People feel a strong sense of commitment to the group.		There is little personal commitment to the group.
Communication with others is poor		Group communicates well with rest of organization

It is worthwhile taking this opportunity to pursue the point made about the personalities and attributes of team members since an important starting point for creating an effective team is to examine its make-up and the characteristics of its membership. The model provided by Belbin (1981) for doing so is extremely useful. From the findings of his research with teams of managers, he concluded that the mix of personal characteristics in a team is a key determinant of its effectiveness. If teams do not display this mix they are less likely to be effective in their task. He suggests that people have intuitive ways of acting in team situations, generally based on their self-perception. To understand why some teams are likely to perform better than others, Belbin draws a distinction between team members' 'functional roles' and their 'team roles'. These distinctions are set out below.

- Functional role – The functional role is essentially the one that a person is paid to fulfil. It is in general what we are selected to do largely because of our ability, experience and skills.

• Team role – The team role is the additional role we play. It is our tendency to behave, contribute and interact in certain ways and is more likely to be shaped by our personality and learned behaviour than by technical skills and knowledge we have.

It should be pointed out that there are limitations to applying Belbin's model to schools, where teams are less clearly defined and staff selected mainly for their subject specialisms. Nevertheless, the model still has much to offer team leaders. Belbin identified nine team roles and showed how it is possible to use these roles to analyse a team and predict how well it will work. The teams that are likely to perform best are the ones that have the most appropriate blend of team roles. This does not mean that it is necessary to have nine team members, simply that the roles should be represented as fully as possible. The nine team roles, together with their typical characteristics, positive qualities and allowable weaknesses (the price one pays for the strengths they bring to the team) are shown in Table 2.3.

You and your colleagues may or may not be surprised to discover what your preferred team role appears to be. Is this role the one that you consistently play, whatever team or context you are in? For example, are you always the person who has the bright ideas (shaper) or insists on following an issue or task right through to the end (completer/finisher)? Given the fluidity of teams in schools, it is highly desirable that team leaders and team members are able to adjust their role according to their perception of what needs to be done in any particular team. We also change roles over time, depending on how long we have been in a team and the roles adopted by other team members. The most successful teams then are those whose members have a complementary range of skills and abilities, plus the flexibility to adapt roles and behaviour to circumstances and contexts. Table 2.4 shows examples of primary and secondary roles that members of a school's senior management could adopt, together with their psychological and social attributes.

Point for reflection

Use Belbin's descriptions of team types to help you recognize the characteristic behaviours displayed not only by yourself but also by colleagues in your team. Think about ways in which you might use these strengths to increase the performance of your team. How crucial is it to take account of the 'allowable weaknesses' column when attempting to do this?

Team leaders should also be aware that teams go through a series of clear stages in the move to full effectiveness. Bruce Tuckman (1965) provides a definition of these stages of team development (Table 2.5).

A successful team knows which stage it is operating in, and manages transition through the different stages adeptly. The central principle in team building is to minimize the time spent **FORMING** and **STORMING**, to make **NORMING** as powerful as possible and to devote the maximum amount of time to **PERFORMING**. There are no short cuts!

Table 2.3 Characteristics of team types (adapted from Belbin, 1981)

Role types	Role characteristics	Positive qualities	Allowable weaknesses
Company worker or implementer	• translates ideas into practice • gets on with the job • works with care and thoroughness	• organizing ability • common sense • integrity • hard working • loyal • self-disciplined	• lack of flexibility and adaptability
Chair or coordinator	• controls and coordinates • driven by objectives • utilizes team resources	• enthusiastic • assertive • flexible • strong sense of duty	• not really creative or inspirational
Shaper	• pushes to get the job done • inspires • makes things happen	• drive • enthusiasm • challenges roles • commands respect • intolerant of vagueness	• needs to be in charge • impulsive • impatient • unduly sensitive to criticism
Innovator or plant	• advances new ideas • synthesizes knowledge	• intelligence • imagination • creativity • unorthodox	• prefers ideas to people • ignores practical issues
Resource investigator	• identifies ideas and resources from outside the team • questions and explores	• very good at networking • positive • cheerful • sustains the team	• lacks self-discipline • impulsive • ignores practical issues
Monitor/ evaluator	• critical thinker • analyses ideas • constantly reviews the team	• interprets complex data • judgement • hard-headed • objective	• over-critical • negative • sceptical and cynical
Team worker	• socially oriented • loyal to the team • promotes harmony • perceptive of feelings, needs and concerns	• stable • extrovert • good listener • promotes strengths • underpins weaknesses	• indecisive • can forget a task
Completer/ finisher	• drives for task completion – on time and according to specification	• obsessed with detail • strong sense of purpose • driven by targets	• anxious • compulsive • can lower morale
Specialist	• has prior knowledge and specialist skills	• contributes specialist expertise as team input	• tends toward narrow and overly specific view

Table 2.4 Example showing primary and secondary roles adopted by members of a school's senior management

Post	Primary role	Secondary role
Head	Resource investigator (people-oriented)	Coordinator (people-oriented)
Deputy	Implementer (action-oriented)	Monitor/evaluator (cerebral)
Deputy	Coordinator (people-oriented)	Team worker (people-oriented)
'Senior' teacher	Completer/finisher (action-oriented)	Implementer (action-oriented)
'Senior' teacher	Team worker (people-oriented)	Plant (cerebral)

Table 2.5 Four stages of team development (adapted from Tuckman, 1965)

What tends to happen?	Stage of development	What is the danger for the leader?
If people do not know each other, they are self-conscious, impersonal, guarded, testing, somewhat stilted in conversation and sometimes even embarrassed	**FORMING (Ritual sniffing and getting acquainted)**	Slow, self-conscious operation by the team may mean that you are obliged to take many team decisions. However, too much domination by you at this stage will inhibit development. Aim to move your team rapidly out of this phase by seeking opinions, discussing roles and procedures
	⇩	
Team members battle for role. There are difficulties, confrontations, conflicts of opinion, infighting. The activity swings between lively debate and feeling stuck. Some will appear to be opting out, demotivated and divisions may occur in the team.	**STORMING (Infighting and trying out ways of working)**	If members are not encouraged to accept each other's strengths and weaknesses, you will be papering over the cracks with surface agreements. The latent conflict will appear later when the team is under pressure. Bring conflict out into the open and treat it as a problem to be solved.
	⇩	
Planning starts. Systems and procedures begin to get established. The team is getting organized. Working standards and norms are laid down. Roles are clear. Skills are developing. Leadership patterns are emerging.	**NORMING (Experimenting and getting settled)**	The team is gathering strength from creating norms and from trial runs. Be prepared that, if these meet with disaster, the team may lose confidence and regress to the 'storming' stage.
	⇩	
Solutions to problems emerge. More output in less time. Quality of team outcomes improves. Decisions translated into action. Team more resourceful and supportive of each other and confident.	**PERFORMING (Maturing and achieving excellence)**	This effective team needs worthwhile challenges or it will become frustrated. Also, be aware of overconfidence.

Point for reflection

If you have not already noticed your team displaying some of Tuckman's character-istics of team development, you may find it useful to observe the efficiency with which it moves through the four stages of forming, storming, norming and performing. What determines or influences the efficiency with which the team moves to the performing stage? What strategies might you employ to ease the way to greater team maturity?

Teams can be formed by as few as two, and as many as you like! Beyond, say, twenty-five the task of team leadership becomes more complex, but there are numerous examples, in all walks of life, where teams operate successfully in much greater numbers e.g. orchestras. More important than the size of the team is its pattern of working – the way in which team members settle to perform their tasks.

WHAT SHOULD I ATTEMPT TO DO TO BUILD TEAMWORK?

Effective leadership has to include the twin skills of team building and team maintenance. It is worth remembering that the dynamic nature of any group may accelerate or decelerate more quickly than that of any individual within it. Team building is not always easy and most teams need to be developed through several stages before becoming totally effective. To build a team you might find it useful to follow the guidelines summarized in Figure 2.2 and explored below.

Figure 2.2 **Building a highly effective team**

Point for reflection

Review your current strategies for building your team in order to maximize their effectiveness. Identify specific examples of where you have successfully:

- freed up members of your team to encourage their creativity;
- helped team members develop personally and professionally;

- achieved team purpose by meeting agreed objectives;
- encouraged and supported team members;
- built and maintained good working relationships with team members;
- modelled desirable behaviour.

Free up team members

Freeing up team members (Figure 2.3) means encouraging them to release their imagination, their creativity, their potential, and their skills for the benefit of the school and the team. Effective team leaders achieve this in a number of ways whilst still retaining overall responsibility. For example, by:

Figure 2.3 **Freeing up team members**

Not blaming team members for errors

Few schools, or areas within them, will readily admit to adopting a blame culture, but such cultures do exist. Having a no-blame culture does not mean lack of accountability or indifference when things go wrong, nor does it mean excusing recurring errors. Effective team leaders make every effort to promote a culture that encourages team members to identify, rectify and then learn from errors made.

Encouraging team members to develop new ideas, take decisions and see them through

The liberating culture, referred to above, promotes conditions within the team that encourages team members to contribute ideas and solutions to problems. Nothing is more heartening for a member of staff than to have ideas requested, listened to, and then implemented. Staff need to feel that they can contribute even 'off the wall' ideas generated by their knowledge and inspiration, and completely new ideas generated by imagining the future as it could be.

Listening to staff

To be listened to is to be valued. Stephen Covey (1992) recognizes the importance of listening to understand when he says: 'seek first to understand, then to be understood'. Listening for understanding requires that we remove the clutter in our minds – the clutter associated with our experiences, relationships, abstract thoughts – so that we are not distracted from genuine active listening (a theme pursued in Chapter 9).

Facilitating full and open communication

There are times when team leaders will find it extremely difficult to be totally open about issues because of personal confidentiality and sensitivity. In these circumstances it is wiser to be upfront and offer an explanation. Without transparency, people make up their own version of events, which can frequently be negative – even inaccurate. Besides, the truth – or a version of it – will normally escape anyway. To be effective, team leader communication with team members needs to reinforce the context, values and purpose of team activity. In other words, context offers the 'what' (what we are trying to achieve); values the 'how' (how we intend to go about things and how we work with each other); and purposes the 'why' (why we are investing all this effort).

Operating systems based on trust

Leadership research (e.g. Bennis and Nanus, 1985; Covey, 1989; Bush and Middlewood, 1997; Day, Hall and Whitaker, 1998) shows that people are inspired by leaders who create trusting relationships. Trust is invariably established when team members feel valued and worthwhile and team leaders can achieve this by showing respect for their colleagues (e.g. by arriving punctually), being genuine (e.g. by not being two-faced), and above all by demonstrating understanding (e.g. by empathizing with colleagues).

Encourage and support team members

Schools are highly pressurized places where encouragement and offers of support from team leaders go a long way to promoting team ethos and a culture of mutual support (Figure 2.4). Successful team leaders achieve positive team culture by:

Accepting responsibility for the actions of team members

Accepting responsibility is very important for the purpose of building trust with team members. Whenever possible, team leaders should avoid distancing themselves from team members who make errors. Team leaders may not be personally accountable for the error but may well be responsible for why it happened and they are certainly accountable for the resulting action. The little word 'we' becomes highly significant here.

Giving praise

Try never to be accused by team members of not saying 'thank you'. The important thing to remember in praise is to 'catch people doing things right

Figure 2.4 **Encouraging and supporting team members**

and well'. It is important to praise genuinely for results or effort above the norm, for new ideas, or simply a special moment or behaviour you wish to reinforce. As important is never to overdo the praise – it loses its meaning and will be seen as trite.

Recognizing and acting to minimize team member stress

Stress in some people is often the result of a combination of high challenge in their work but low support to help them achieve it. Figure 2.5 shows the likely effect of imbalances between appropriate support and challenge.

Continued high stress leads to 'burn out', while continued apathy can lead to 'rust out'. Team leaders can help team members by doing all that they can to:

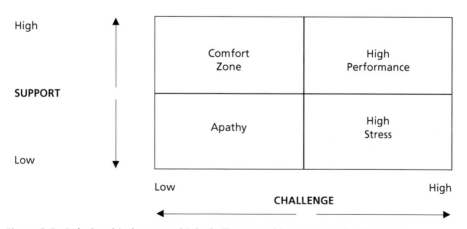

Figure 2.5 **Relationship between high challenge and low support leading to stress**

- encourage staff to do less to achieve more – helping them manage time and priorities; and

- prevent outside influences from causing anxiety.

Supporting team members

There is a close link between the support provided by team leaders and the previous point related to stress. Supporting staff is a vital part of building trust within the team and of achieving high-level performance. Team leaders need to be aware of the different levels at which support can be provided. It is apparent that support is required when things start to go wrong, or when there is underperformance.

Regularly meeting with individual team members to clarify direction

The purpose of these one-to-ones is to check on work progress, priorities and issues. Meeting face to face is very helpful in maintaining a team member's sense of value and importance. It allows for swift support, corrective action and the opportunity to extend success. Performance management reviews are a highly effective means of providing regularized meetings for this purpose.

Achieve team purpose

Getting results and achieving team objectives (Figure 2.6) are, of course, important for the success of the school as a whole as well as for the self-esteem of the team. Working with their team, effective team leaders will be:

Figure 2.6 **Achieving team purpose**

Achieving results

When it comes to achieving results we are talking on two levels. First, the need for the team leader and the team to be successful in achieving their key purposes, as presented in the form of targets and objectives. Secondly, and possibly more importantly, to be gaining significant outcomes, e.g. examination results, SATs, development of pupils' skills and attitudes.

Agreeing targets and objectives with individuals and with the team as a whole

Targets and objectives are important to achieve success, for motivation and a sense of accomplishment. Targets that are challenging provide an opportunity to raise performance beyond current standards. Involving teams and team members in setting targets is worthwhile since it stands a better chance of gaining their commitment.

Consulting those affected before making decisions

Genuine consultation with team members has the potential to gather a host of new ideas, as well as insights into their thinking, feelings and priorities.

Willing to take unpopular decisions in order to move forward

Taking difficult decisions may be shied away from or done in such a way as to mask those aspects likely to be unpopular, such as dealing with someone whose performance is unacceptable. Team leaders have a responsibility to communicate with team members in such a way as to inform them of where they stand. The key principle is to remember that gaining and holding team members' respect is more beneficial than trying to be popular.

Regularly communicating an inspiring view of the future

Quite clearly, what is being described here is 'vision' – that rich commodity that gives us our purpose and our framework for operating. An overall vision for the school may be broken down into global, team and individual ones.

Constantly seeking to improve the way things are done

The role of team leaders is to encourage team members to believe that 'if better is possible – good is not good enough'. Not only is it about learning from mistakes, it is also about learning from success.

Help people to develop

One of the most important considerations for team leaders is in developing individuals and teams (Figure 2.7). Effective team leaders will seek ways of:

Encouraging others to learn

A great deal continues to be said about schools as learning organizations. What seems to have become clearer is that the experience that staff bring to a role has to be supplemented by their ability to learn and think ahead. There is an interesting view, held by some theorists, that suggests that the most effective

Figure 2.7 **Helping people to develop**

ways of learning are not simply trying to transfer knowledge and ideas from one person's head to another, but through experiential learning or stepping into the unknown to try something out. Whatever your thoughts on this, try using the simple technique of asking three key questions in relation to what you do:

- What went well?
- What went less well?
- What do we want to see/see done differently next time?

Encouraging people to work together as a team

The team leader's role is to frame the team's objectives and to ensure that team members are clear about the shared values that influence the way they operate. Effective teams are characterized by team leaders who:

- set high expectations of output and conduct;
- model good behaviour;
- articulate an inspiring vision;
- get people to contribute and act responsibly for the benefit of the team;
- deal with problem team members; and
- share success and learning in public.

Meeting regularly with the team as a whole to review progress

Team meetings are one of the key ways to share and reinforce points about direction and progress. This does not replace one-to-one meetings, but team meetings give the team leader the opportunity to talk with the team face to face, gain immediate feedback and ensure that everyone is at the same level of understanding on important matters.

Taking time to develop and coach team members

The investment of time to help staff develop will pay huge dividends. Coaching is about helping people to learn (Chapter 10 is devoted to coaching).

Dealing effectively with breaches in standards of behaviour

The most important thing for leaders to do in this situation is to act early – the longer breaches apply, the greater the damage done and the more difficult it is to correct matters. To minimize the chances of such breakdowns occurring, team leaders would be wise to:

- document important procedures;
- check that team members understand what is required;
- check that what is being asked of staff is realistic; and
- that staff have the resources and training to deliver.

Treating other people's mistakes as learning opportunities

We all make mistakes and it may be a cliché to treat them as learning opportunities, but like many clichés it has a solid grounding in reality. The best way to deal with this kind of situation is to:

- correct the mistake;
- review how and why it happened; and
- agree action that will prevent it from recurring.

Model desirable behaviour

Nothing does more to establish team culture and trust than team leaders who are prepared and able to model the behaviours and attitudes they really want (Figure 2.8). Effective team leaders make efforts to:

Actively encourage feedback on their own performance

Feedback, though not always palatable, is valuable to everyone and team leaders need to set an example by encouraging it as a normal part of working. A vital first step to being a team leader is to know yourself and paying close attention to feedback is a crucial aspect of this.

Work on their own learning and development

Such is the pace of change in our schools that team leaders need to work on their own learning as a strong example for team members. Seeking out continuing professional development opportunities is an important strategy for team leaders.

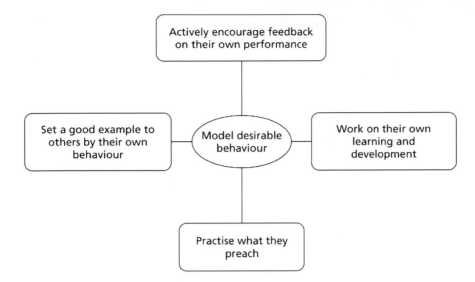

Figure 2.8 **Model desirable behaviour**

Practise what they preach

The impact of the team leader's behaviour is huge – it is so closely aligned with integrity and trust. The difficulty for team leaders is that staff take great notice not only of what is said but also of what is done. As Gandhi said, 'We must be the change we wish to see in other people'.

Set a good example to others by their own behaviour

There are countless examples of how team leaders might do this. The more obvious ones tend to include: being consistent about important standards and procedures, e.g. marking, meeting deadlines for reports; genuinely listening to people; avoiding double standards.

Build and maintain working relationships

A recurring theme through this book is that effective team leadership relies on creating a climate of trusting relationships (Figure 2.9). Within schools, particularly at a time of exponential change, team leaders are certain of nothing more than a few months ahead. In asking people to bring about continuous improvements, team members have to trust the intent of their leaders. Effective team leaders make progress here by:

Not putting self-interest before the interests of team members

Team leaders derive huge satisfaction from the success of their team. By looking after team members' interests there is every likelihood that they will be more successful and have stronger feelings of support and loyalty to their leader.

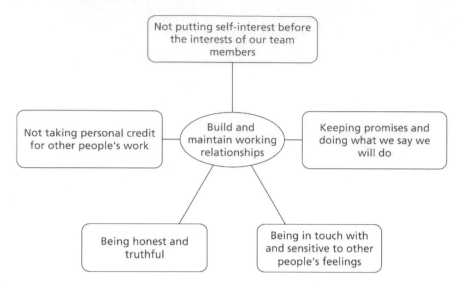

Figure 2.9 **Build and maintain working relationships**

Keeping promises and doing what we say we will do

Real trust can only be built up over a period of time. This means that team leaders should show commitment to their team members by being reliable and dependable, especially after having made promises and given assurances.

Being in touch with and sensitive to other people's feelings

Daniel Goleman's (1996) work on emotional intelligence is particularly significant here. Real engagement and motivation comes more from the heart than the head, and the heart is about feeling.

Being honest and truthful

Despite the difficulties that might arise, leaders need to be genuine about what they discuss with their team, even and especially when it is at all negative. Effective team leaders seek collaboration – they open discussion with the relevant people rather than indulge in clandestine or corridor conversations.

Not taking personal credit for other people's work

Failure to do this is a quick and sure way to destroy trust. Credit needs to be provided where credit is due.

HOW CAN I GAUGE THE QUALITY OF THE TEAMWORK?

Effective teams pause, once in a while, to review the quality of their teamworking. Very often, teams work well enough to do the job but never really unlock the potential that they have within themselves. The following checklist helps teams review their effectiveness:

Use the descriptions below to score your personal assessment of the way that the team is working currently. Invite each member of the team to rate each lettered statement 0 to 5. Share your individual assessments by calculating the average score you gave to each statement. The team should then reflect on the results and develop an action plan to improve overall team effectiveness.

Scoring

5 strongly agree – team fully operational and exceeds the description
4 agree – team operational and meets all or nearly all aspects of the description
3 slightly agree – team operational but incomplete
2 slightly disagree – team nearly operational but some way to go
1 disagree – quite a long way to go
0 strongly disagree – quality of teamwork seriously underdeveloped

Team purpose	a.	The team has a clear vision and direction	5 4 3 2 1 0
	b.	The team has success criteria that are challenging and meaningful	5 4 3 2 1 0
	c.	The team understands how its work fits into the bigger strategic picture	5 4 3 2 1 0
Team leadership	d.	The leader balances appropriate direction with support and openness	5 4 3 2 1 0
	e.	The leader discusses key issues openly with the team	5 4 3 2 1 0
	f.	The leader delegates appropriately to team members	5 4 3 2 1 0
Understanding differences	g.	Team members understand their roles and where these overlap with others' roles	5 4 3 2 1 0
	h.	Team members are clear about what is expected of them individually	5 4 3 2 1 0
	i.	Team members are clear about what individual strengths they each bring	5 4 3 2 1 0
Team processes	j.	Team meetings are effective	5 4 3 2 1 0
	k.	The team has found and implemented more effective ways of working	5 4 3 2 1 0
	l.	The team has an efficient process for solving problems and reaching decisions	5 4 3 2 1 0
Team communication	m.	Team members feel that their ideas and inputs are listened to by the rest of the team	5 4 3 2 1 0
	n.	Differences and conflicts are resolved openly and constructively	5 4 3 2 1 0

	o.	Team members' interaction is open and honest	5 4 3 2 1 0
Team relationships	p.	There is trust and openness between team members	5 4 3 2 1 0
	q.	New members feel valued and quickly become productive members of the team	5 4 3 2 1 0
	r.	The team takes responsibility for its successes and failures and avoids blaming others	5 4 3 2 1 0

SUMMARY SELF-REVIEW

Spend a little time considering and then responding to the following review questions:

1. When I talk about the work of the team, do I say 'my' and 'I' or 'our' and 'we'?

2. What kind of risks am I prepared to take in pursuit of team goals?

3. How do I earn the respect of the team?

4. What signs are there that the team trusts me?

5. How even-handedly do I deal with team members?

6. To what extent do I value face-to-face contact with team members?

7. How remote am I in my style of communication?

8. What do I do to remain optimistic about progress?

9. How do I help the team to acknowledge realities without alienating them?

10. How do I show that I am genuinely pleased with the team's successes?

11. How readily do I accept mistakes as learning opportunities?

12. To what extent do I see errors as an opportunity to apportion blame?

13. How willingly do team members contribute their ideas?

14. How confidently do team members make decisions about the work that is done and use their discretion to make improvements?

Action planning

Having spent some time reviewing your approach to leading and developing teams, identify some actions that you might take to strengthen your current approach.

3 Motivating Members of the Team

The ability to motivate others is – next to delegating – perhaps the most quintessential management skill. It involves not only the provision of an amenable working environment, but also of intrinsic interest, responsibility and recognition.

(Lessem, 1991)

INTRODUCTION

Today's increasing pressure on schools to perform well means that a highly motivated staff is vital to achieve improvements. Therefore, learning how to motivate the team has become an essential skill for team leaders. For good reasons, motivation has become one of the buzz-words of modern leadership and management. How often do we hear, and possibly use, phrases like: 'He lacks motivation', 'Pat really knows how to motivate her team – they'll do anything for her', 'We need to motivate the staff . . .'? Yet, like all human states, motivation is both highly individual and complex and there is a difference between what motivates people to perform at a high level and what leads to indifferent performance. This chapter looks at the nature of motivation and describes how to make sense of what is known about motivation theory in order to create and sustain a positive team attitude. By responding to the following likely questions from team leaders, the chapter offers advice and techniques to put these aspects into practice:

➢ What is motivation?

➢ Why is motivation so important to the work of a team?

➢ How does a team leader recognize the needs of team members? In what ways can motivation theory help me?

➢ How do I set about trying to understand staff attitudes and build their motivation?

➢ How do I deal with demotivated people?

➢ When I've got them motivated, how do I keep them that way?

WHAT IS MOTIVATION?

Like many theories about management and leadership, 'motivation is a contested concept with no agreed, single definition' (Law and Glover, 2000). Despite difficulties over its precise nature, motivation is pivotal for team leaders because it is what makes people want to do things. Motivation is what makes them put real effort into what they do. Clearly, motivation varies in its

Table 3.1 Indicators of present and absent motivation

Signs that motivation is present	Signs that motivation is absent
• High performance • High results being consistently achieved • Energy, enthusiasm and determination to succeed • Unstinting cooperation to overcome problems • Willingness to accept responsibility • Willingness to accommodate necessary change	• Apathy and indifference towards the job • Poor record of timekeeping and high absenteeism • Exaggeration of the effects/difficulties encountered in problems, disputes and grievances • Lack of cooperation in dealing with problems or difficulties • Unjustified resistance to change

nature and intensity from one person to another, depending on the particular range of influences impacting on them at any given time. We all recognize motivation by its presence but, more often, we are aware of its absence. The attitudes and behaviour of team colleagues are a good indication of their motivational state. Table 3.1 details some of the tell-tale signs of 'present' and 'absent' motivation.

In the current climate of rapid change and ever-increasing pressure in schools, effective team leaders need to be both well-organized managers and highly skilled in understanding people's basic requirements and behaviours in the workplace. So much of the team leader's success relies on gaining commitment, nurturing talent and ensuring that team members are motivated and productive. All of this does not come about magically or mysteriously. It requires effective communication and trust between team leaders and their staff colleagues.

Point for reflection

Use the following checklist of questions to try to identify the varying kinds of motivated behaviour in your team. Try asking these questions with each member of your team in mind.

- Do they appear to be comfortable when required to work alone?
- Are they eager to accept responsibility?
- Do they enjoy a good argument?
- Having started a task, do they see it through?
- Are they sensitive to the feelings of others?
- Do they interact with others?
- Are status symbols especially important to them?
- Do they respond positively to difficult or challenging circumstances?
- Do they work better when there are deadlines to be met?
- Do they seek positions of authority?
- When given responsibility, do they set and meet standards of high performance?
- Do they try hard to get personally involved with senior staff?
- Are they especially eager to become their own boss?
- Are they regularly involved in team projects?
- Do they try to take control?

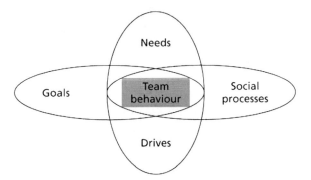

Figure 3.1 The importance of motivation to the work of the team

- Do they try to get as much feedback as possible?
- Do they try to establish harmonious relationships?
- Do they attempt to offer assistance even when not asked to do so?

WHY IS MOTIVATION SO IMPORTANT TO THE WORK OF A TEAM?

Despite the difficulties of being precise about the nature of motivation, the concept is critical for team leaders since it concerns:

- the goals that influence team behaviour;

- the thought processes that we use to identify our needs and drives towards particular goals and decisions; and

- the social processes that influence our behaviour patterns (see Figure 3.1).

Motivation is vital in any job if people are to give of their best. If we assume that staff are given adequate opportunity to perform well and have the necessary skills, then it is their motivation that determines whether they are truly effective or not. Your team members are undoubtedly a critical resource – as well as being a costly one – and no matter what the degree of sophistication we achieve in terms of technology, we will always be reliant on human factors to maximize their skills and attributes.

HOW DOES A TEAM LEADER RECOGNIZE THE NEEDS OF TEAM MEMBERS? IN WHAT WAYS CAN MOTIVATION THEORY HELP ME?

People have a variety of needs, many of which go far beyond basics such as good working conditions, job security and fair pay. These have to be met, but doing so will not in itself give satisfaction. Failures with the basic needs nearly always explain dissatisfaction among staff. On the other hand, meeting people's higher-level needs such as pride in their work and sharing in the

Higher
needs

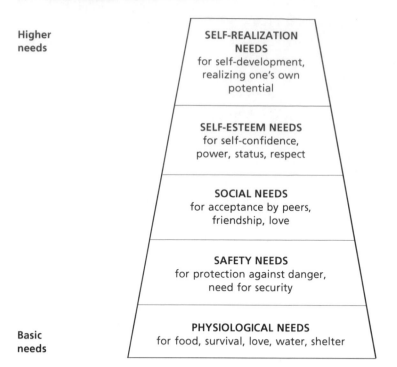

Basic
needs

Figure 3.2 Maslow's hierarchy of needs

goals of the school or the department, though a lot more difficult, invariably leads to satisfaction. Research into people's behaviour, dating from the 1940s, has suggested that people are motivated by a range of needs, both at work and in their personal lives. There are a number of theories about what motivates individuals to work harder. Each has different implications for how you work as a team leader to motivate those for whom you are responsible. Several motivation theories work on the assumption that given the opportunity and the right prompts, individuals work well and productively. Effective team leaders remain constantly alert to what these prompts might be for individual team members. Three of the most influential theories are those of Maslow, Herzberg et al. and McGregor.

Maslow's hierarchy of needs

The clinical psychologist Abraham Maslow believed that all people have needs that they wish to have satisfied. He grouped these needs into a five-stage 'hierarchy of needs' (Figure 3.2), starting with the basic needs for food and shelter and culminating in higher level self-actualization or self-fulfilment needs.

> A musician must make music, an artist must paint, a poet must write, if he is to be ultimately happy. What a man can be, he must be. This need we may call self-actualization . . . It refers to the desire for self-fulfilment, namely the

tendency for him to become actualized in what he is potentially . . . the desire to become more and more what one is, to become everything that one is capable of becoming.

(Maslow, 1943)

According to Maslow, the needs are tackled in order: as you draw nearer to satisfying one need, the priority of the next one becomes higher. He also proposed that, once a need has been met, it is no longer a prompt. In schools, for example, the Maslow hierarchy is particularly relevant because individuals do not just need money and rewards; they also need respect and interaction. When agreeing roles and objectives and organizational structures it is worth bearing in mind the full range of needs in the Maslow hierarchy. Some people may put self-actualization before satisfying lower order needs. Some people may even experience all needs in the course of one day. The theory is not without its problems since, in applying this theory in schools, we seek to satisfy many of our needs outside the workplace.

The two-factor theory of Herzberg et al.

Herzberg, Mausner and Snyderman (1959) developed a two-factor theory for motivation based on 'hygiene factors' and 'motivators'. By hygiene factors (Table 3.2) they refer to basic human needs at work which, in themselves, do not motivate, but their absence causes significant dissatisfaction. Some of these factors, e.g. parking space, holiday entitlement, office space, can be viewed as trivial, whereas pay, finance and resources are important hygiene factors.

The second of Herzberg et al.'s two factors is a set of 'motivators' (Table 3.3) that actually drive people to achieve. These are what team leaders should aim to provide in order to maintain a satisfied workforce. Motivators are built around obtaining growth and self-actualization from tasks.

Table 3.2 Hygiene factors (based on Herzberg et al., 1959)

Hygiene factors	Descriptions
Salary and benefits	Income, fringe benefits, bonuses, holidays, etc.
Working conditions	Working hours, workplace layout, facilities, equipment, etc.
Organizational policies	Rules and regulations; formalities and informalities, etc.
Status	Rank, authority, relationship to others, etc.
Job security	Degree of confidence employee has regarding continued employment
Supervision and autonomy	Extent of control that an individual has over the content and execution of the job
Relationships at work	Level and type of interpersonal relations within the work environment
Personal life	Time spent on family, friends and interests

Table 3.3 Motivators (based on Herzberg et al., 1959)

Motivators	Why they work
Achievement	Reaching or exceeding task objectives is particularly important because the onwards and upwards urge to achieve is a basic human drive. It is one of the most powerful motivators and a great source of satisfaction.
Recognition	The acknowledgement of achievements by others (at a senior level especially) is motivational because it helps to enhance self-esteem. For many staff members, recognition may be viewed as a reward in itself.
Job interests	A job that provides satisfaction for individuals and groups will be a greater motivational force than a job that does not sustain interest. As far as possible, responsibilities should be matched to individuals' interests.
Responsibility	The power to exercise authority and power may demand leadership skills, risk-taking, decision-making, and self-direction, all of which raise self-esteem and are strong motivators.
Advancement	Promotion, progress and rising rewards for achievement are important here. Possibly the main motivator, however, is the feeling that advancement is possible.

Table 3.4 Theory X and Theory Y assumptions (based on McGregor, 1960)

Theory X assumptions	Theory Y assumptions
• Most people inherently dislike work and will avoid it if possible. • People must be coerced, controlled, directed or threatened with punishment to get them to put in adequate effort at work – they are self-centred and lack ambition. • People prefer to be directed, wish to avoid responsibility, have relatively little ambition and, above all, want security.	• People are, by nature, physically and mentally energetic. • People do not need to be externally controlled or directed. They will exercise self-direction in pursuit of objectives to which they are committed. • People will seek and accept responsibility under the right conditions. • People have the capacity to exercise a high degree of creativity, imagination and ingenuity.

McGregor's Theory X and Theory Y

Douglas McGregor (1960) proposed that motivation is influenced by two sets of contrasting assumptions about people and work (Table 3.4). He suggested, albeit over-simplistically, that managers make either Theory X or Theory Y assumptions about the way others behave.

McGregor believed that Theory Y brought about more effective leadership, although he did concede that there were occasions when Theory X behaviour might be appropriate. If team leaders choose either of these sets of assumptions, there may be a tendency for team members to respond to the way they are led, for example, if team members believe that they are not being trusted they may behave in a less trustworthy way. As team leaders we should make every effort to avoid perpetuating Theory X thinking patterns – limited and routinized job activity. Instead we need to promote Theory Y behaviour in order to encourage creativity.

Point for reflection

Using the theories described above, look in detail at your current role and responsibilities. Identify factors in your work associated with satisfaction and dissatisfaction. You may want to compare your findings with others, including members of your team.

HOW DO I SET ABOUT TRYING TO UNDERSTAND STAFF ATTITUDES AND BUILD THEIR MOTIVATION?

To inspire people to work – individually and in teams – in ways that produce the best results, team leaders need to tap into their own personal motivational forces. The art of motivating people starts with an understanding of colleagues' behaviour and then learning how to influence that behaviour. Recognizing certain behaviours and the reasons behind them are important. Team leaders can do this by:

- listening carefully to what is being said;
- interpreting what is said correctly; and
- reading the body language being presented.

By employing the above strategies, you will become aware of motivational behaviour, that is, the way staff:

- guard each others' interests;
- freely volunteer their services and ideas;
- react to being asked to undertake new or additional tasks; and
- show, through their expressions, that they are visibly happy in their work.

Point for reflection

Think of an occasion when you successfully employed the skills of listening, interpreting and reading body language to understand and influence a team colleague's motivational behaviour.

We all suffer from insecurity at some time in our lives. The anxiety we experience say, as a result of our excessive workloads, our subsequent inability to meet deadlines, the pressures of preparing our students for SATs and public examinations, can often add to that insecurity. To build our motivation and thus our confidence we need:

- our contributions to be appropriately recognized and acknowledged;
- to be invited to perform high-level tasks; and
- to be supplied with accurate information.

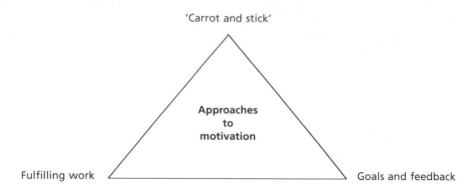

Figure 3.3 **Approaches to motivation (based on Armstrong, 1988)**

However, it is important that team leaders understand 'who they are' and their attitudes towards team members. Our attitudes towards others are influenced by our experience and will shape the way in which we behave towards the people we meet. Various strategies can be employed by team leaders for encouraging motivation. Armstrong (1988), proposed three approaches to motivation (Figure 3.3) while conceding that each has its merits and its deficiencies:

- The 'carrot and stick' approach – based on the notion that people work for rewards: the better the incentive, the harder people are likely to work.

- Motivating through the work itself – based on the notion that offering people fulfilling work will raise their level of satisfaction, thus improving their performance levels.

- The 'one-minute-manager' system – based on the notion that you should set goals for staff, give them positive feedback when they perform well, and negative, but sensitive, feedback when they do something wrong.

Point for reflection

Review your experiences of one or more of Armstrong's approaches to motivating staff. Which ones have worked most effectively? Why do you think this is?

Because it is the responsibility of team leaders to do all that they can to motivate their teams, they are best placed to create the climate in which people will 'grow' and want to give of their best. It is true that there are certain factors outside some team leaders' span of control or influence, e.g. pay, status, terms and conditions of employment. Yet they can provide the recognition, respon-sibility, and challenging work that represent the most powerful motivating factors. With this in mind, it is important for team leaders to remember that staff:

- like to be consulted about what they have to do – just being told what to do does not generate feelings of ownership for a particular policy or action;

- like managers who are willing to listen – feeling that their views are of no significance is demotivating;

- appreciate being seen as valuable individuals with specialist skills – being seen as a mere cog in the machine, easily replaced by other cogs, does not build self-esteem;

- respond to sensitive managers – heavy-handed use of authority is often counter-productive;

- perform better when they enjoy their work and feel relaxed – managers who can spread good cheer and empower will help to motivate them;

- whose successes are recognized become more successful and more motivated – praise is important.

It has been said that there are four kinds of people in the world:

- People who watch things happen

- People to whom things happen

- People who do not know what is happening

- People who make things happen

If you are to be a team leader that makes things happen through and with others, you will need to be aware of how you can get your team to work willingly and well to achieve team goals. Among the strategies available to team leaders are those shown in Table 3.5.

HOW DO I DEAL WITH DEMOTIVATED PEOPLE?

However hard you try to prevent staff demotivation, you will not always be successful. Selecting ways of dealing with demotivated people depends on the situation and it is important to analyse each situation to gauge whether the cause is attributable to stress, emotional issues, physical illness, the nature of the job itself, or the person's approach to it. The most helpful advice here is: ask. Talk to the person in order to identify where the problem lies and tailor the remedy to the cause. In summary:

- stay calm and collected, however emotional the person might become;

- try to establish the reasons for their dissatisfaction as fully as possible;

- listen carefully to what they have to say;

- try to agree a resolution;

- ensure that you get feedback from the person before the discussion ends to avoid further misunderstanding; and

- offer him/her further opportunities for discussion.

Table 3.5 Strategies for building motivation

What to do	How to do it
Make team members feel valued	• spend time getting to know people and then support them • be considerate and fair • listen to people • regularly monitor their work • show an interest in what is important to them • create an atmosphere of approval and cooperation • ensure that they understand the importance of their contribution to the team and to the school
Provide opportunities for development	• communicate clearly and don't be frightened by debate • set standards for the team • agree performance management objectives with each team member • provide training and coaching • use their expertise to train others • make best use of their individual and combined skills • increase the level of consultation and discussion, particularly at times of change
Recognize achievements	• recognize expertise and appreciate the work done • recognize and praise success, and build on it • report regularly on team progress and successes • make good use of ongoing performance review meetings
Provide challenge	• set and communicate team objectives • delegate authority and responsibility as well as tasks • encourage ideas and allow team members the responsibility for implementing them

Point for reflection

Below are two case studies of teachers who, for varying reasons, have seen their motivation levels drop in recent years. What suggestions do you have about what might be done to help either, or both, of them to achieve greater satisfaction from their work?

Jan Watson is 46, and has worked at Caswell Primary School for the past 14 years. She joined the staff soon after qualifying as a teacher, following a period of time spent as a librarian. Almost all of her teaching has been with children in Years 5 and 6. The school has about 340 children. Originally it served a mining community, which has since been integrated into a new estate housing both private and local authority residents.

Jan regards herself as part of the backbone of the school. She is firm on discipline. She takes little part in the extra-curricular life of the school, apart from a little help with concerts. Jan is reluctant to attend professional development courses, especially those held out of school. She contributes very little during training days. Her attitude to the curriculum and to new teaching methods is conservative and she has opposed the school's initiatives in relation to ICT. She seems to see value in the literacy hour. She was given a management allowance for Maths many years ago, and still continues as subject coordinator, although the deputy headteacher does most of the work.

She is a stickler for form-filling, registers, marking work on time and for formal courtesies. She appears to be regarded well by pupils, parents and ex-pupils. The quality of her teaching is variable and can range from very good to very ordinary depending on her state of mind and the topic. At one point in her recent performance review with you, her team leader, she commented that she was:

> very depressed at the slack standards in the school. It's a sign of the times of course – sloppy dress, bad timekeeping, untidy writing. It's a general drop in standards throughout society. I can't be doing with all these new-fangled management gimmicks. What we need are clear rules so that the children – and the parents for that matter – know what's what.

John Francis is 44 and Deputy Head of Clandon High School. He was unsuccessful in becoming head of the school just under two years ago, when the previous incumbant retired. His resentment at not getting the job increasingly shows through. He is ambitious for the status of headteacher. He has applied for a number of posts for which he has usually been interviewed but not appointed.

The school is an 800-pupil, mixed comprehensive, serving a mixed catchment – as near to a truly comprehensive intake as you might get. He has the reputation of being a hard worker for the school on committees and in out-of-school activities. He gets on quite well with the new headteacher. At the moment he feels that his efforts have not been rewarded, and has spells of cynicism. Among his comments are:

> There are too many passengers in education. People should be paid for what they do, and sacked if they can't do it. I'm all for merit payments, such as more money for extra work and bigger differentials for responsibility. It's time we sorted out the idle and useless from those who are prepared to work for it. I'm after promotion – outside the school, of course.

Despite being a good administrator, he does not seem to relate well to people. Staff, and even some of the pupils, appear to find his personality unsympathetic and lacking in understanding and perception.

WHEN I'VE GOT THEM MOTIVATED, HOW DO I KEEP THEM THAT WAY?

It is one thing successfully to raise the motivation levels of your staff, it is quite another to ensure that things stay that way. Varying working conditions, improving systems and valuing your staff's contribution are ways of doing so. It is important to remember that the majority of those we work with want to feel good about their work and their school. This is a natural drive and one which all team leaders need to nurture. Effective team leaders select trusted individuals to talk to informally about the general mood, as well as developments that affect motivation.

Point for reflection
Think of someone for whom you have worked and who has been able to 'press your motivation buttons'. How have they achieved this – what strategies, techniques and

ploys have they used to spur you on to even greater efforts? Which of these might become part of your repertoire of motivational techniques?

SUMMARY SELF-REVIEW

Spend a little time considering and then responding to the following review questions:

1. To what extent do I persuade and influence my team as opposed to demanding what I want?

2. How do I try to ensure that the work is enjoyable for my team?

3. How effectively do I use non-verbal means to communicate and to influence decision-making?

4. How confident am I that I give my team full and frank information whenever possible?

5. How well do I gauge the attitude of team members?

6. How aware am I that I apply Theory Y principles rather than Theory X, or vice versa?

7. How successful am I at involving team members in issues as early as possible?

8. How readily do I give reasons for my actions if I disagree with team members?

9. How effective am I at seeking consensus and encouraging others to do likewise?

10. How readily do I blame others for team failures?

11. How successfully do I achieve a balance between firm control and giving the team independence?

12. How readily do I attempt to improve my motivational skills?

13. How effective am I at removing obstacles to team performance?

14. How clear am I about my benchmarks when gauging team successes?

15. How effectively do I organize the work so that team members can own and complete entire tasks?

16. How successfully do I encourage team members to act on their own initiatives?

17. How well do I confront difficult 'people' decisions?

18. How readily do I act to avert or settle disputes and personality clashes within the team?

19. How well do I recognize and praise work done by the team?

20. How alert am I to team members who are not using their full potential?

Action planning

Having spent some time reviewing your approach to motivating your team, identify some actions that you might take to strengthen your current approach.

4 Managing Time and Priorities

I love deadlines. I like the whooshing sound they make as they fly by.
(Douglas Adams, writer and producer)

INTRODUCTION

Team leaders, are expected not just to plan and prioritize their own work but to be responsible also for what their team does. In addition, there is an expectation that they are able to balance their work and home life. So, managing time and priorities is vitally important from both a personal and professional standpoint. According to the ancient Greek philosopher Theophrastus, time is 'our costliest expenditure'. We want, and need, to use our time efficiently in order to accomplish all that we have to do. With this in mind, what can we do to help us cope with the increased levels of demand on our time and attention? Truthfully, very little on a 'macro' level, but probably a lot more on the 'micro' level. This chapter offers you some techniques to plan your time and prioritize more effectively using the following questions:

➢ What is time management?

➢ How do I know whether I have a time management problem?

➢ So, where does my time go?

➢ How can I deal with the time thieves?

➢ How can I exercise greater control over my personal work patterns?

➢ Am I alone in having a problem managing my time? What can I do about it?

➢ How can I re-establish some control over my management of time?

➢ What is the best way of dealing with the paperwork?

➢ What other ways are there of improving my personal organization?

➢ How important is it to use technology to help me manage my time?

WHAT IS TIME MANAGEMENT?

Time management is actually self-management – it is about using time effectively to achieve tasks. Increasingly, everyone has to face up to the problem of not having enough time. Clearly, there cannot be any more time than there is! As much as we might wish otherwise, there cannot be more than 24 hrs in a day or 7 days in a week. So, we have to make optimum use of the time we have available. Successful time management:

- enables you to gain a better perspective of pending activities and priorities;

- ensures more opportunities to be creative (being proactive rather than reactive);

- helps you deal with, reduce and often avoid stress;

- helps you gain more leisure time; and

- enables you to attain your objectives consistently and systematically.

Point for reflection

Some of the above points regarding time management are brought home in the following illustration:

One day an expert in time management was speaking to a group of business students. As he stood in front of the group of high-powered overachievers, he said, 'Okay, time for a quiz.' Then he pulled out a one-gallon wide-mouthed Mason jar and set it on the table in front of him. Then he produced about a dozen fist-sized rocks and carefully placed them, one at a time, into the jar. When the jar was filled to the top and no more rocks would fit inside, he asked, 'Is this jar full?' Everyone in the class said, 'Yes.' Then he said, 'Really?' He reached under the table and pulled out a bucket of gravel. Then he dumped some gravel in and shook the jar, causing pieces of gravel to work themselves down into the space between the big rocks. Then he asked the group once more. 'Is the jar full?' By this time the class was on to him. 'Probably not,' one of them answered. 'Good!' he replied. He reached under the table and brought out a bucket of sand. He started dumping the sand in the jar, and it went into all of the spaces left between the rocks and the gravel. Once more he asked the question, 'Is this jar full?' 'No!' The class shouted. Once again he said, 'Good.' Then he grabbed a pitcher of water and began to pour it in until the jar was filled to the brim. Then he looked at the class and asked, 'What is the point of this illustration?' One eager beaver raised his hand and said, 'The point is, no matter how full your schedule is, if you try really hard you can always fit some more things in it!' 'No,' the speaker replied, 'that's not the point. The truth this illustration teaches us is: If you don't put the big rocks in first, you'll never get them in at all.' What are the 'big rocks' in your life? Your children, your loved ones, your education, your dreams, a worthy cause, teaching or mentoring others, doing things that you love, time for yourself, your health, your significant other? Remember to put these BIG ROCKS in first or you'll never get them in at all. If you sweat the little stuff (the gravel, the sand) then you'll fill your life with little things you worry about that don't really matter, and you'll never have the real quality time you need to spend on the big, important stuff (the big rocks). So, tonight, or in the *morning, when you are reflecting on this short story, ask yourself this question: What are the 'big rocks' in my life? Then, put those in your jar first.**

(Cheryl Drangstveit, Business Support Specialist, Women's Business Center)

Give some thought to what are the 'big rocks' in your life – professional and personal.

HOW DO I KNOW WHETHER I HAVE A TIME MANAGEMENT PROBLEM?

This is a basic but very important question to ask – 'Do I have a problem managing time?', 'When will I know that I have a time management problem?' You are likely to need to reassess your time management if you are responding 'yes' to most of the situations outlined in Table 4.1.

Table 4.1 Assessing the extent of your time management problem

Am I?	Yes	No
failing to meet deadlines regularly?		
putting off things that I ought to do?		
spending too long on telephone calls?		
having insufficient time to think?		
unsure where my time goes?		
achieving less than I think my efforts deserve?		
unable to say 'no' to people?		
attempting to achieve perfection rather than excellence, and achieving neither?		
arriving home late because of 'pressure of work'?		
involved in meetings that are not productive?		
spending insufficient time with my family?		
thinking too much about work problems at home?		
forgetting important professional/personal details?		
failing to keep promises?		

Point for reflection

Have you ever wondered how much your time is worth? This is an interesting calculation, as well as sobering, especially when you are attempting to find out if you are spending your time profitably. To get the most reliable figure, use the following calculation to work out how much your time at school costs per hour and per minute.

$$\frac{1.5 \times \text{annual salary}}{\text{working hours/year}} = \text{cost per hour}$$

---

*www.onlinewbc.gov/docs/manage/TimeManagement.html

$$\frac{\text{cost per hour}}{60} = \text{cost per minute}$$

Use these figures to analyse the relative costs of some of the typical daily activities you undertake.

SO, WHERE DOES MY TIME GO?

No one has total control over their time – someone or something will always make demands. Team leaders, for example, have huge competing demands made upon their time. One of the highly significant factors affecting the majority of team leaders in schools is that much of their time is regulated. For example, they have class responsibilities and a fixed commitment to teaching via an organized timetable. This means that leadership and management functions have to be carried out at other times, for example:

- before the start of the school day;

- during breaks and lunchtimes;

- during non-contact time (where it exists) in the school day;

- when the pupils have left for the day;

- during dedicated or protected time in the school day;

- during statutory closure days; and

- in 'private time' such as evenings, weekends and holidays.

Even within structured time, there are opportunities to select which tasks or activities to handle and what priority to assign each of them. It helps us to make better use of the time available if we can become more fully aware of the current habits and attitudes that shape our use of time:

Point for reflection
Keeping a daily time log is, in itself, further consuming your time, but it is an exercise that does provide valuable insights into your time expenditure on particular activities. Try to take a typical school day and compile a straightforward time log by dividing your day into 30-minute intervals and record precisely how you spend your time. Try to maintain your time log for at least a week – longer if at all possible.

Using the findings of your time-logging exercise, review your use of time by responding to the following questions. Think of ways in which you might be able to make better use of time.

On what activities do I seem to be spending *less* time than I would like?
On what activities do I seem to be spending *more* time than I would like?
What proportion of my time is spent in reacting to crises and on unplanned events?

What activities lend themselves to delegation to team members?
To what extent are my working arrangements causing ineffective use of
time e.g. office, equipment, facilities, filing systems?

Point for reflection

The first step in managing time is to establish just where your time goes. The Roman
philosopher Seneca suggested that 'part of our time is stolen from us, or else we are
cheated out of it'. What or who steals your time? Make use of the following
self-assessment chart to help identify your time thieves.

	Almost always true	Frequently true	Sometimes true	Almost never true
The telephone constantly interrupts me and the conversations are usually longer than they need to be				
Numerous visitors from outside or within the school often keep me from carrying out my work				
Meetings frequently last much longer than planned, with little in the way of satisfactory outcomes for me				
I usually put off weighty tasks because I can't seem to concentrate for long enough				
I lack priorities and I try to perform too many tasks at once – I can't seem to concentrate on what's important				
I can only meet my schedules and deadlines under pressure – something unexpected always comes up				
There is too much paperwork, which means that my desk is never orderly or tidy				
There is often too little communication with others resulting in delayed information and misunderstandings				

Delegation of tasks almost never works out – I end up taking care of things myself				
It is difficult for me to say no when others ask me to do things				
I don't have any clear professional or personal goals, so I don't see much meaning in what I do every day				
Sometimes I lack the necessary self-discipline to carry out what I had planned to do				

HOW CAN I DEAL WITH THE TIME THIEVES?

The only sensible way for us to make better use of our time is to analyse how we currently use it and then consider ways in which we can redistribute it more efficiently. This means learning to handle our time thieves. The activity you have just undertaken is likely to have given you a pretty clear indication of who and what are your time thieves. The more common 'top 10' are set out in Table 4.2, together with some suggestions as to how they might be avoided or made less intrusive on your time.

HOW CAN I EXERCISE GREATER CONTROL OVER MY PERSONAL WORK PATTERNS?

Each of us has a natural daily rhythm to our energy patterns. For instance, we experience troughs of low energy at some times in the day and peaks of high performance at others. Some people are at their best in the morning, others peak in the afternoon. Within the context of the role of team leader, it is important to recognize and come to terms with our personal rhythm so that we can work with, rather than against, it.

Point for reflection

How well do you know your energy patterns and your natural daily rhythm? When in the day do you normally feel most tired? When in the day do you feel most alert and energetic?

Take a look at the chart shown in Figure 4.1, which is completed for you to illustrate the energy patterns of an unidentified staff member. Note how this individual's energy levels change at points A, B and C. What conclusions might you draw?

Draw up your own chart to show how your energy levels vary during a typical working day. Assign a number between 5 and −5 to your performance at 30 minute

Table 4.2 Dealing with time thieves

Time thieves	Possible solutions
Poor meetings	• Look for alternatives, e.g. e-mails, memos, informal contact. • Draw up an agenda, review it at start of meeting. • Always start and finish on time. • List time to be spent against each agenda item in relation to its importance. • Chair firmly. • Use flip chart/ whiteboard to keep focus. • Identify decisions needed on agenda. • Use flip chart to build consensus. • Use standard outline for recording minutes. • Check progress at pre-determined intervals. Note: Meetings management is dealt with fully in a later chapter (Chapter 6).
Interruptions	• If you have one, use your secretary's skills to filter your telephone calls and requests for your time. • Try standing up when you take calls or when people drop in on you, as opposed to sitting. The more comfortable you are, the greater the tendency to prolong the conversation. • If the conversation is going on too long, try to separate chat from information. • Say: 'I only have 5 minutes because . . .' Indicate an ending using phrases like: 'Before we finish . . .'
Lack of objectives, priorities and planning	• Try using a planner or developing your diary as a daily, weekly, monthly planner based on key tasks. • Organize uninterrupted time to plan at fixed point during the week. • List your tasks and prioritize them for the days and weeks ahead. Set yourself some deadlines for their completion.
Indecision and procrastination	• Putting things off is not unusual human behaviour. Typically, we put off tasks that are boring, difficult, unpleasant or onerous. Yet, they will have to be dealt with. Try: – setting a deadline to complete the task and sticking to it – building in a reward system or a personal incentive – arranging with someone to check with you on a routine basis about progress on tasks you tend to put off – doing these tasks first thing in the day and getting rid of them – dividing the task into small pieces and dealing with one at a time.
Crisis management	• Unexpected events do occur that must be handled then and there. Those that are beyond our control need to be handled in an orderly, methodical way. Some crises, however, are the result of something that was not dealt with satisfactorily in the past. It is possible to minimize future crises by reviewing past ones and looking for patterns and factors that can be minimized or eliminated.

- Try planning before you act. Check the feasibility of your plan by setting realistic deadlines by planning backwards from the time of completion.
- Build in realistic cushions in case things go wrong. Anticipate crises by doing 'worst case analyses' and having contingency plans in place. Ask yourself:
  - What could go wrong?
  - When might it occur?
  - What will I do about it?
- Ignore minor problems. If possible, delegate problems that your colleagues can deal with.

Inability to say 'no'

- At some point, we all have demands on our time that we find difficult to accommodate. Here is where learning to say 'no' really helps. Saying 'no' does not necessarily offend. One approach is to offer and alternative:
  - 'I can't deal with that this minute, but I'll have a look at it when I've finished this.'
  - 'I'll be glad to handle that for you. But, I can't get to it until I finish what I'm doing. It'll be about 2.30 this afternoon.'

Lack of self-discipline and involved in too many things

- 'Go public' on your time plans with colleagues so that you feel more obligation to implement them.
- Initiate a team development activity on time management so that your team's awareness and willingness to cooperate is raised.
- Sharpen up your time planning.
- Do fewer jobs better.

Too much paperwork

- Sharpen up your time planning.
- Standardize your written communications.
- Colour-code documents according to their importance or urgency, or to signify the required action, e.g. reply needed, file, technical information.
- Examine and agree with colleagues the criteria for using meetings, memos, telephone calls, informal contact.
- Consider when to circulate documents, such as minutes, as opposed to displaying them in a predetermined place in the staff room or team office.

Visitors

- Controlling time taken by visitors requires both courtesy and judgement. A useful strategy if you need to meet with a colleague briefly is to visit their work area. This way you can simply excuse yourself when your task is completed. It is often more difficult to get people to leave your area than it is for you to leave theirs.

Mail

- Unsolicited mail is never-ending. If someone else sorts your mail, give some guidelines on what you want to see separated into piles, such as 'information only' and 'action'; what should be routed to others; and what should be binned. If it's your responsibility, you can use a similar system, but you will probably need to be quite strict.

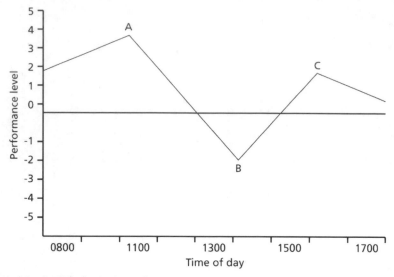

Figure 4.1 A typical energy cycle

intervals during the working day (0 represents an average level of performance) and mark it on your chart. Join the marks A, B, C, etc. to illustrate your energy cycle. What conclusions might you draw? What implications are there for the way in which you might manage your time in future?

One obvious implication of understanding your energy cycle is that you try to carry out the most demanding tasks at times in the day when you are at your physical and mental peak. For example, if you get enjoyment from jogging early in the morning, try to ensure that you complete most of your really important tasks early in the day.

AM I ALONE IN HAVING A PROBLEM MANAGING MY TIME? WHAT CAN I DO ABOUT IT?

Surveys carried out by a range of organizations, such as The Industrial Society, have found that colleagues working in a variety of employment areas experience difficulties at some time in managing their time. The key findings suggest that employees complain of being:

- overloaded with work – and having to rely on overtime to complete the work;

- stressed – having to deal with too many things at once, tight deadlines, etc;

- controlled by their work – reacting to work pressures instead of taking the initiative;

- sidetracked in their work by a range of distractions – for example, protracted meetings; and

- unable to establish a balance between work and leisure time.

There are some people who are capable of doing more, of being more organized, than others. It is not as though those people have found more time – what they are able to do is to manage the time they have more effectively. To do so, they have taken account of a number of factors, not least, their *personality* and what *motivates* them. Our personality has an effect upon our ability to manage the time we have available. There are three characteristics that influence this ability:

1. Are you a **perfectionist**? If you are, you:

   - are likely to be worried about what other people think of you;

   - may put off doing things in case you fail;

   - may work endlessly at something, always trying to improve it that little bit more;

   - always think that you could have done something better; and

   - may take a long time to do either simple or relatively unimportant things.

Being a perfectionist uses up endless amounts of time. Winston Churchill was once asked by someone how to spell perfection. The answer he gave was P-A-R-A-L-Y-S-I-S. Not being a perfectionist does not mean being slapdash – there is a middle way, which involves doing things as well as possible in the time available.

2. Are you a **workaholic**? If you are, you:

   - love working very hard;

   - set goals which you often fail to reach;

   - can't stand being inactive;

   - feel guilty if you relax or slow down;

   - prefer doing to reflecting;

   - accept more work than you can handle;

   - have difficulty balancing your personal and professional life; and

   - are often stressed.

Workaholics get a lot of things done. The question is, do they get them done well and do they get them done with the cooperation of others?

3. Are you almost always in permanent **crisis**? If you are, you:

   - feel you have little control over outside events;

   - are unlikely to plan well – including ignoring warning signals, overloading your schedule, not planning far enough ahead;

- may be poor at estimating deadlines;
- enjoy the feeling of pressure; and
- find it hard to face up to the facts of a situation.

HOW CAN I RE-ESTABLISH SOME CONTROL OVER MY MANAGEMENT OF TIME?

Time management is a personal process and must fit your style and circumstances. It takes a strong commitment to use time effectively. It is about achieving tasks but it is also about prioritizing tasks and organizing yourself well (Table 4.3).

Table 4.3 Two ways of establishing control over your management of time

Prioritizing tasks	Organizing yourself
<ul><li>making lists</li><li>evaluating</li><li>sorting tasks into categories</li><li>judgement</li></ul>	<ul><li>diaries</li><li>action lists</li><li>booking time for reactive tasks</li><li>thinking</li><li>planning</li></ul>

Prioritizing tasks

Prioritizing means selecting important tasks from those waiting to be carried out. The trick is to identify the ones that are important from those that merely seem to be important. In Drucker's words, 'It is better to do the right work (=effectiveness) than to do the work right (=efficiency)' (1988). There is only one way to judge: does the task contribute towards achieving the objectives of the school as a whole and/or of the team? If it does, it is an important task. By ranking your tasks in order of importance, you ensure that:

- you work on important tasks first;

- if necessary, you work on tasks according to their urgency;

- you concentrate on just one task at a time;

- you handle the tasks more effectively in the time scheduled;

- the set objectives are attained as effectively as possible under the circumstances;

- all tasks which can be performed by others are put aside and delegated;

- at the end of the planned period (e.g. a working day, half-term), the most important matters are, at any rate, taken care of; and

- the tasks by which you and your achievements are judged are completed.

Point for reflection

Spend a little time thinking about some of your uncompleted tasks. Use the priority matrix below to sort them.

1. high importance/high urgency
2. low importance/high urgency
3. high importance/low urgency
4. low importance/low urgency

ABC Analysis

The ABC analysis is a simple but effective tool for prioritizing your tasks. It requires you to perform a value analysis of the use of your time in which you show the relative proportions of actual time spent on very important (**A**), important (**B**) and less important (**C**) tasks. Studies have shown that actual time spent on a task does not correspond to the value of the activity (Table 4.4).

Table 4.4 Setting priorities using the ABC method

Tasks	Value of the activity %	Actual use of time %
A Tasks: these are the most important – must do – tasks. They can be carried out properly only by you (i.e. they cannot be delegated), and are of the utmost importance in fulfilling your role and responsibilities	65	15
B Tasks: these are tasks that you 'should do'. They are of medium value and may contribute to improved performance but are not essential or do not have critical deadlines	20	20
C Tasks: these tasks are 'nice to do' tasks because they are often interesting or fun. They could be eliminated, postponed or scheduled for slack periods	15	65

Time is often wasted on trivial tasks (C), while the few essential tasks (A) are often neglected. The key to successful time management is to give the scheduled activities a clear priority by ranking them according to an ABC classification system. The ABC analysis does not imply that *only* A tasks should be performed and C tasks may be dispensed with completely, but rather that all activities should be brought into a balanced relationship with each other, given the correct status, and organized into a daily work sequence by means of setting priorities. Because priorities change from day to day, today's B may become tomorrow's A as an important deadline approaches. Likewise, today's A may become tomorrow's C if circumstances change. In practice, ABC analysis functions best when you:

- schedule only one or two A tasks per day;

- earmark a further two or three B tasks; and

- set some time for C tasks.

Point for reflection

List some of your uncompleted tasks, including those that are merely objectives in your overall plan. Use the summary chart in Figure 4.2 to help you allocate A for very important, B for important, and C for trivial/routine tasks.

Organizing yourself

Organizing yourself means keeping control of diaries, action lists, your desk, your briefcase, and the key areas of your life. It means thinking and planning, even booking time to spend time with yourself. The **LEADS** method is relatively simple and requires an average of 8 minutes of planning time per day.

- **L**ist tasks, activities and deadlines;

- **E**stimate time needed;

- **A**llow time for unscheduled tasks;

- **D**ecide on priorities;

- **S**can scheduled tasks at end of day.

Table 4.5 shows the LEADS method in more detail.

Table 4.5 The LEADS method for organizing yourself

List your tasks, activities and deadlines	• List jobs to be done, and the deadlines for this week or month. • List unfinished work from the previous day. • List new work for the day. • List deadlines to be met. • List telephone calls to be taken care of. • List correspondence to be taken care of. • List regular activities e.g. SMT meetings, teaching commitments.
Estimate the time needed to complete your tasks	• Be careful not to overplan. • Calculate time spent. • Set time limits. • Eliminate interruptions.
Allow buffer time for unscheduled tasks	• Schedule only 60 per cent.
Decide on priorities	• Set priorities. • Be more selective. • Delegate.
Scan scheduled tasks at end of day	• Tackle it or cancel it.

WHAT IS THE BEST WAY OF DEALING WITH THE PAPERWORK?

We all comment on the amount of reading matter that comes into school – it is overwhelming. It seems unlikely to change, however, and so the most

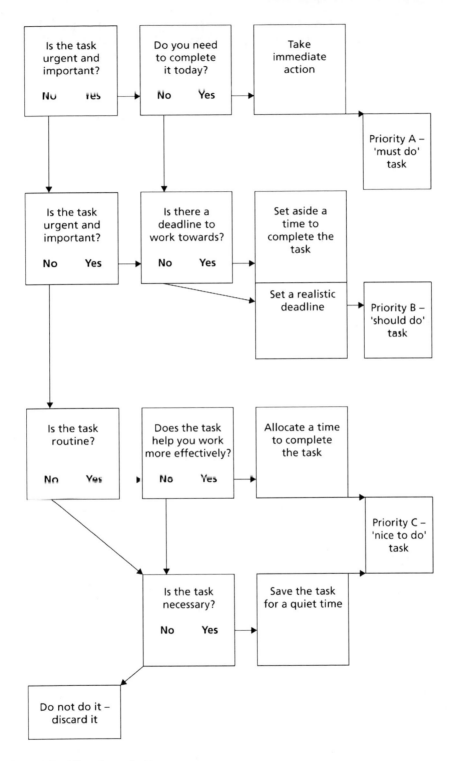

Figure 4.2 **Allocating priority**

important question is, how can we read what *has* to be read most efficiently? Our experience tells us that different people have different reading skills. This is because some people:

- are easily distracted when they read;

- have different reading skills to cope with different types of literature;

- can read at speed;

- can grasp the overall concept of an article or document easily; and

- can skim read.

Paperwork has a tendency to take over in at least three places: the in-tray, the desk and the briefcase. Try to make it the rule to touch each piece of paper once only. Sort everything into three piles using **AID**:

- **A**ction – set up an action file that holds papers that you are working on currently.

- **I**nformation – important information usually needs to be retrieved at some point so a good filing system is crucial. A good filing system is one that allows you to find things in seconds rather than minutes. However, keeping filing systems efficient requires you to remove outdated information at least once per term. A good test of a filing system is whether your team members would be able to find urgent information in your absence.

- **D**iscard – a great deal of what arrives in your tray tends to be irrelevant. When you are satisfied that items really are of no interest or are irrelevant, bin them or shred them.

WHAT OTHER WAYS ARE THERE OF IMPROVING MY PERSONAL ORGANIZATION?

There are a variety of other ways for keeping on top of the administration load:

- *Study a colleague who seems to be particularly well organized* – never underestimate this way of learning new techniques. We all work with colleagues who have strengths in areas different from our own. You may already be thinking of someone whose personal organization is well advanced and from whom you could pick up some worthwhile tips for improving yours.

- *Use your diary effectively* – ensure important deadlines and appointments are recorded, and include notes in your diary at a suitable point to allow you enough time to prepare for the event.

- *Select an organizer/time planner to make regular schedules* – transfer key events from your diary onto a term or year planner to provide you with an 'at a glance' facility. This should enable you organize your work more effectively and anticipate bottlenecks.

- *Draw up a daily list of things to do* – it is useful to have a list of jobs to do for each day. It is more helpful than trying to memorize all that you have to do. The physical act of ticking off completed tasks is also quite satisfying.

Point for reflection

Mrs Anderson is Head of the Humanities Faculty and a 6th Form Tutor. She has a number of tasks that need her attention. How would you advise Mrs Anderson to plan her day in order to use her time efficiently? What guidelines would you offer her for the most effective use of her time in the future? Her timetable for the day is shown in the chart.

0800	Arrive in school	1150–1300	Y10 Geography
0845–0910	Tutor Group Registration	1300–1400	Lunch break
0910–1015	Non-contact time	1405–1410	Tutor Group Registration
1020–1125	Y12 Geography	1415–1520	Non-contact time
1125–1150	Break	1530–1700	Faculty meeting

There are 18 tasks on her list:

1. See House Head re complaints about behaviour of Y10 in History.
2. Write reference for Mr Chalmers (Geog. Dept.).
3. Start Y11 Mock Exam (not supervise) at 0915.
4. Speak to the Headteacher about Faculty capitation.
5. Prepare thoughts for Faculty meeting.
6. See Mrs Johnson about Mock History paper for tomorrow's exam.
7. Pop out to the bank.
8. Remind everyone about Faculty meeting at 1530 today.
9. See Head of Art at break re collaboration over topic in Y9.
10. Photocopy material for Y12 Geog. lesson.
11. Contact parent beginning of afternoon re 'A' Level student's repeated failure to hand in work.
12. Complete supplementary requisition for school finance officer.
13. Pop into Orienteering Club meeting during lunch.
14. Mark remaining Y13 essays before tomorrow.
15. Check with Mrs Marsh (DHT) on dates for Field Work visit.
16. Telephone for dental appointment
17. Arrange classroom observation for Miss Dunelm's appraisal.
18. See Macmillan rep. during lunch.

HOW IMPORTANT IS IT TO USE TECHNOLOGY TO HELP ME MANAGE MY TIME?

Few of us can make effective use of our time without some help from information technology. Try to build your skills in this area – it will pay dividends. Increased knowledge and skills will improve your efficiency and effectiveness when it comes to:

- designing systems for storing information;
- developing ways of classifying your information;
- labelling your documents clearly and logically;
- using e-mails for communicating with a range of others; and
- searching for information speedily.

SUMMARY SELF-REVIEW

Spend a little time considering and then responding to the following review questions:

1. How regularly do I analyse my use of time in order to find more efficient ways of working?

2. To what extent do team members feel that they should not make work decisions themselves but should bring problems to me?

3. How much of my time is spent doing things for others in the team that they could/should do for themselves?

4. How regularly do I have unfinished jobs accumulating, or difficulty in meeting deadlines?

5. How common is it for me to spend more time working on details than on planning and supervising?

6. How strongly do I feel the need to keep close tabs on the detail if a team member is doing a job well?

7. How likely am I to work at details because I enjoy them, although someone else could do them well enough?

8. How inclined am I to try to keep a finger in everything that is going on?

9. How inclined am I to lack confidence in my team members' ability with the result that I am afraid to risk letting them take over more details?

10. Am I a perfectionist with details that are important for the main objectives of my position?

11. How readily do I admit to needing help to keep on top of my role and responsibilities?

12. How guilty am I of neglecting to ask the team for their ideas about problems that arise in their work?

13. What is my technique for dealing with my mail?

14. How effective am I at 'skim-reading'?

15. How effectively do I deal with interruptions?

16. How do I limit the duration of telephone calls?

17. How do I keep the contents of my in-tray to a manageable size?

18. How effectively do I delegate to and follow-up tasks with colleagues?

19. Do I make a list of things to do each day? How well do I stick to it?

20. How successful are my efforts to keep in touch personally with my team?

Action planning

Having spent some time reviewing your approach to managing time and priorities, identify some actions that you might take to strengthen your current approach.

5

Encouraging Team Development through Effective Delegation

To him, delegating work is rather like donating blood – frightening to contemplate, messy in the giving and, worst of all, entailing a personal and irreplaceable loss.

(Quoted in Goodworth, 1985)

INTRODUCTION

Delegation is a skill of which we have all heard – but which few really understand. It can be used either as an excuse for dumping tasks onto the shoulders of colleagues, or as a dynamic tool for motivating and training your team to realize their full potential. Delegation underpins a style of management that allows your team to use and develop their skills and knowledge to the full potential. Yet, it is not instinctive human behaviour. This chapter looks at the form and function of delegation; its importance as a skill for team leaders; and ways in which it can be approached in schools.

➢ What exactly is delegation?

➢ What if I am not comfortable with delegating my work?

➢ Are there different kinds or levels of delegation?

➢ How does the delegation process work?

➢ How can I delegate successfully?

➢ What are the links between people's learning styles and delegation?

➢ How do I conduct a successful briefing meeting?

➢ How can I build in effective and responsive monitoring and support?

➢ What part does coaching have to play in delegation?

WHAT EXACTLY IS DELEGATION?

At times, we all need to pass on work and responsibility to our colleagues. Delegation is an important technique to acquire, not simply because it relieves us of workload, but because it can be used as a way of motivating those with whom we work. Delegation occurs, therefore, when the team leader chooses to entrust a team member with a specific task that he or she could have retained for him or herself. It is the art of getting a job done by the person best able to do it, in the time available, and is primarily about entrusting your authority to others. This means that they can act and initiate independently;

and that they assume responsibility with you for certain tasks. If something goes wrong, you remain responsible since you are the manager; the skill is to delegate in such a way that tasks get done but do not go (badly) wrong. Such a task could be a 'one-off', or one that might become a regular feature of that person's work.

Point for reflection

To help you arrive at your own view of what is meant by delegation, consider the following arguments in favour of delegation. With which do you most strongly agree?

- *'Delegating eases the strain on us as team leaders and creates time for more important tasks.'*
- *'Delegating helps to exploit the specialized knowledge and experience of team members.'*
- *'Delegating helps to promote and develop the abilities, initiative, self-reliance and competence of team members.'*
- *'Delegating often has a positive effect on the motivation and job satisfaction of team members.'*

WHAT IF I AM NOT COMFORTABLE WITH DELEGATING MY WORK?

Many of us have very mixed feelings about giving away parts of our work to someone else. This is partially explained by the fact that each job we undertake comprises three elements – responsibility, authority and accountability:

- **Responsibility.** If we are responsible for the job it normally means that we are the ones who actually carry it out.

- **Authority.** This is the decision-making part of the job. We make decisions about the way the job is done.

- **Accountability.** This is the ownership part of the job. We are accountable, even if we didn't actually perform the task ourselves.

Therefore, effective delegation involves giving someone else responsibility for the job, the authority to take decisions and, in the short-term, protecting them by retaining accountability. It is this last element that helps us draw the distinction between delegating and 'dumping' – allocating tasks that we are not terribly fond of. There are several common barriers to delegation, generally stemming from our concerns.

'What if something goes wrong'

Quite frankly, there is no way of knowing whether your team colleagues will get it wrong if they are never given the chance to get it right. Obviously, you will not delegate a task to anyone if you genuinely believe that the risk of failure far outweighs the probability of success. In most cases, you will need to give team colleagues the benefit of the doubt. You may even need to think back to times in your career when your team leaders showed faith in you.

'I'll be quicker doing it myself'

It is quite easy for each of us to believe this. Undoubtedly, as a team leader, and by virtue of your experience and the expertise gained over time, you will probably be more effective at many tasks than your team colleagues. However, taking this approach will lead to a massive workload. Apart from your not being in a position to spend more time on higher-level tasks that only you can and should do, how will your staff ever become proficient if they are not given the opportunity? Try to think of the coaching that you will have to do as an investment in your colleague's future. Also, any coaching that you do need not absorb a vast amount of your time if you spread it over two or three short sessions.

'I've always looked after this myself'

This is what we tend to say when we operate within our own comfort zone. We hang on to these jobs for many reasons, e.g. they are high-profile jobs and get us noticed; they are areas of work in which we have real skills and we get confidence from doing them well; to lose them might make us personally and professionally vulnerable. Retaining too many of these areas of work could lead to fossilization – on this basis you will not grow and develop. You may even be overtaken by events!

'My team members are overworked as it is'

The worry of overburdening team members is a significant barrier to delegation. Caring team leaders will want to ensure that colleagues' workloads are not excessive. It is difficult to delegate further tasks to staff members who appear to be working to full capacity already. Rather than retaining these tasks and feeling that you have to do them yourself, try to encourage your team to analyse their own use of time and free up capacity for higher-order activities.

'I feel insecure about asking established team members to take on my tasks'

The challenge for inexperienced team leaders is to master the complex aspects of the process, such as attaining an affective and appropriate leadership style. Frankly, delegation is a self-teaching activity – you develop and perfect the skills through the process itself. Your confidence and abilities increase the more you delegate.

Point for reflection

Take a little time to think about the composition of a team that you lead. Consider the individuals within the team and their potential for benefiting from some level of delegation. The matrix may help you identify the characteristics of your team members.

CAN DO – WILL DO	WILL DO – CAN'T DO
These are ideal team members because they are pleased to accept total responsibility for specific tasks delegated to them. They are also pleased to consult with others and accept appropriate advice.	These tend to be team members who may need quite a bit of encouragement and training to help them overcome their lack of experience before taking on delegated responsibility.
CAN DO – WON'T DO	CAN'T DO – WON'T DO
These team members may well be reluctant to learn or accept the advice of others. They often resent the notion of being delegated to and can be thought of as simply not team players.	The lack of motivation and ability shown by these team members may point to the need for intensive coaching and at worst, capability measures.

ARE THERE DIFFERENT KINDS OR LEVELS OF DELEGATION?

According to Covey (1989) there are basically two kinds of delegation: 'gofer delegation' and 'stewardship delegation'. The former means 'go for this, go for that, do this, do that, and tell me when it's done'. The latter is focused on outcomes instead of methods. It offers team members a choice of how to do things and responsibility for whatever happens. It needs some investment of time to start with, but it is worth it.

HOW DOES THE DELEGATION PROCESS WORK?

Delegation is an art – not an exact science. An important thing for team leaders to remember is that there are no absolute rules that apply to every situation. Nevertheless, as a general guideline, make sure that you **DELEGATE** using the guidance provided in Table 5.1.

HOW CAN I DELEGATE SUCCESSFULLY?

The delegation process (Figure 5.1) begins with analysis – selecting the tasks that you, the team leader, could and should delegate. It will help if you think about the tasks that you are currently engaged in and ask yourself the following questions:

1. Do I *have* to do this task?

2. *Why* do I do it?

3. Should *I* keep it and if so why?

Table 5.1 **The process of delegation at work**

Designate	specific team members to perform specific tasks. If you give open-ended tasks, you'll find yourself filling in gaps. That takes time. Start off with small tasks for each person and work your way to bigger projects. Although some team members will be receptive to taking on more responsibility, others will need time to warm to the idea.
Explain	the nature of the work you have assigned. Even the most skilled team members will need to understand exactly what is expected of them in order to complete the work. Don't make assumptions based on what *you* know about the job. Make sure you cover the fundamentals of the task, as well as the intricate details.
Leave	yourself the option to influence the work. If you are the type of person who wants things done in a very particular way – in your mind, the right way – you should have the right to steer the project when necessary. However, too much control will result in a resentful team member. Even worse, you could end up back where you started: with you doing all the work
Establish	incentives for team members. They may want, and most likely deserve, a fair share of any 'rewards' that are due. For example, the work may count towards some form of accreditation, or there may be local and/or national kudos associated with the work.
Grant	team members the authority to take decisive action. That is not the same as giving them carte blanche to do whatever they please. You can't expect a team member to do a job well if he or she needs to obtain approval every step of the way. Provide some flexibility – but never too much.
Assign	team colleagues tasks that match well with their particular talents and abilities. Consider each person's strengths and weaknesses and their relative experience.
Track	the progress of the work you have assigned. Despite delegating, you still have to ensure that quality standards are met. Delegation does not mean abdication.
Evaluate	the performance of those to whom you have delegated work using the performance management systems within the school. Review the work and offer constructive feedback to your team colleague. Balance the pluses and minuses and focus on the learning.

4. *Who else* could do the job?

5. *Who* could I be training up to do it?

Analyse your time

If you decide to carry out the time analysis activity in an earlier chapter (Chapter 4), it should identify for you the proportion of time you spend on high-level activities that only you can and should do. As a general rule, far more time will have been spent on activities that are routine and could therefore be delegated.

Break down your tasks

List your tasks and group them using, say, the ABC analysis set out in Chapter 4 – those that must be done by you and therefore cannot be delegated (A tasks); those that you could and should delegate (B tasks); and those that do

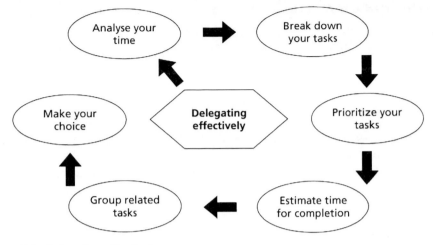

Figure 5.1 **Delegating effectively**

not really need to be done (C tasks). Use this technique for reducing any unnecessary tasks, delegating some and concentrating on tasks that only you can complete (Figure 5.2).

Prioritize your tasks

Once selected, the parameters of the task need to be defined. This will enable you to appoint a suitable team member and to provide him or her with as accurate a brief as possible. You can only make this decision when you have assessed your time and that of your team, and grouped and prioritized activities and tasks.

Estimate time for completion

When delegating tasks you need to have a fairly good idea of how long each task is likely to take to complete. This is an estimate that you can often base on your own experience or on that of others. Try to provide challenging but realistic schedules and deadlines.

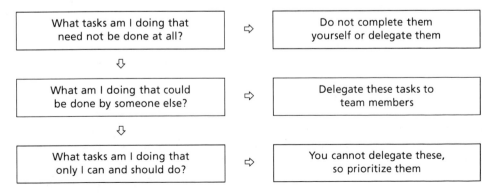

Figure 5.2 **Deciding what to delegate**

Group related tasks

It is likely that the list of tasks to be done will produce activities that are related to each other. It is sensible to delegate groups of related tasks to one person. In this way, you can play to team members' strengths, as well as providing them with continuity and task progression.

Make your choice

Ultimately, the choice of what you delegate, however logical the analysis has been, will have some element of subjectivity.

Once you have selected the task and the individual, you need to work with them to establish the parameters of the job and the level of authority that they will have. They need to be allowed some freedom to carry out the job in their own way. If you just want them to do it how you would do it, then this is another example of 'dumping'.

Point for reflection

Refer to your current list of things to do. Divide these into three categories:

1. Things that only you can do.
2. Things that others could do with little or no help from you.
3. Things that you could delegate but only after extensive preparation and training for the delegate.

For those tasks categorized as (2) or (3), identify a member of your team to whom a task could be delegated. Using the following headings, prepare an action plan:

DELEGATION ACTION PLAN

- Task to be delegated:
- Person who will take responsibility:
- Desired/expected outcome:
- Details of negotiation and briefing to be undertaken with delegate:
- Nature of support being provided:
- Detail of progress monitoring and review:

Point for reflection

There are several levels of authority associated with delegation. The individual could:

- provide you with the information and you decide;
- find out the information, report the pluses and minuses of each decision and you decide;
- recommend action and you decide;
- decide the action and get approval from you;
- carry out the action and report the results to you;
- carry out the action and only report back if something goes wrong; and
- carry out the action.

Which of these levels of authority would you prefer to adopt with your team? What are your reasons?

WHAT ARE THE LINKS BETWEEN PEOPLE'S LEARNING STYLES AND DELEGATION?

Learning is a continual process – sometimes we learn without even realizing it, at other times we make a conscious effort to learn something. In recent years research has reinforced our view that people learn in different ways, and that this can have a significant influence on how readily people respond to delegation. Kolb's (1984) work suggests that to learn we must first have an experience (appeals to activists), then reflect on what happened (appeals to reflectors). Following reflection, we must consider what we have learned and what conclusions we can draw from it (appeals to theorists). Finally, we must then consider how we can apply what we have learned in the future (appeals to pragmatists). Honey and Mumford (1988), for example, demonstrated that there are four styles of learning, summarized in Table 5.2.

Table 5.2   **Four styles of learning (based on Honey and Mumford, 1988)**

Style of learning	Characteristic behaviours
Activist	<ul><li>prefers to get on with the job</li><li>prefers to learn by doing</li><li>will try anything once</li><li>relishes being thrown in at the deep end</li><li>doesn't mind making mistakes but values learning from them</li></ul>
Theorist	<ul><li>likes to analyse situations and behaviour and make philosophical sense of situations, without necessarily needing to prove them empirically</li><li>needs to put learning in context</li><li>learns best through being able to work with principles and theories</li><li>thinks problems through in a logical, step-by-step way</li></ul>
Reflector	<ul><li>spends a lot of time thinking about what has been done and what is to be done</li><li>wants time to absorb learning</li><li>doesn't like being rushed</li></ul>
Pragmatist	<ul><li>main concern is the practical application of what s/he has learned</li><li>learn most effectively when s/he can understand and agree with the practical relevance of the learning</li></ul>

It appears that each of us has a preference for one, possibly two, of these styles. Each of these styles is valid – there is no question of one style being better than the others. Whenever you delegate tasks you will need to consider your own preferred learning style as well as theirs. For example, if you, an activist, delegate a task to a team member whose preferred learning style is a reflector, s/he could easily panic and feel out of their depth. Yet, as team leaders we also have a role in trying to expand our own and our colleagues' learning into areas in which we are less confident; for example, encouraging a theorist (usually over-cautious) to have a go and take risks. A team member might view new tasks using the three 'zones of experience':

- **Comfort zone** – Within the team member's 'comfort' zone are those aspects of their work in which they are quite experienced and proficient.

- **Stretch zone** – In the 'stretch' zone, team members are testing their ability to handle unfamiliar tasks or trying to improve in some aspect of the job which they may not enjoy or value but, nevertheless, cannot escape.

- **Panic zone** – The 'panic' zone takes team members into skill areas that are far beyond their capability.

Point for reflection

Think about the descriptions of the four learning styles and identify which one most closely describes how you learn. If you have a strong preference for one particular style, how would you set out to balance this out by developing other learning styles? Think about which activities will best support your development.

As a team leader, how important is it to provide opportunities for team members to enter the 'stretch zone'? How would you guard against taking colleagues into the 'panic zone'?

HOW DO I CONDUCT A SUCCESSFUL BRIEFING MEETING?

Once you have reached agreement, in principle, to delegating aspects of your work, the time is right to set up a meeting at which you will be able to brief your team colleague. This meeting is vital since it provides team leaders with the opportunity to communicate effectively and ensure the team member's full understanding of the task. This is best achieved by being methodical in your approach and will allow you to:

- explain the task objective clearly;

- state your expectations in terms of deadlines and levels of measured achievement;

- list the steps you think will need to be taken to ensure completion of the task;

- be clear about areas of the brief where flexibility is acceptable, even encouraged, and those which must be followed strictly; and

- check your colleague's understanding of the brief.

You will need to be aware, however, that even the most carefully prepared and well-communicated brief can still result in a lack of full understanding. You can try to avoid this situation by:

- checking with your colleague, throughout the briefing, that things are clear;

- inviting your colleague to check the clarity of his/her understanding with you;

- checking his/her body language, e.g. your colleague's lack of eye contact may indicate that s/he is not in agreement with you, or is having difficulty understanding;

- summarizing the key points of the delegation; and

- reassuring your colleague by building in dates for supportive follow-up meetings.

Your choice of briefing approach will depend on the nature and complexity of the task, the relationship between yourself and your team colleague, as well as your personal style. Don't forget to thank your colleague for taking on the task!

Point for reflection

What is your preferred style for briefing team colleagues? Check your personal approach against the options shown in Table 5.3. In what circumstances would you use any of these options?

Table 5.3 Team briefing styles

Style	Approach	Considerations
Informal	You might say: 'I'd like you to take this on for me when you've got the time.'	Helpful when dealing with staff you know quite well and for delegating less important and straightforward tasks. An oral briefing is usually enough, although follow-up is usually needed.
Formal	You might say: 'I've decided to put you in charge of arrangements for the school's open day for parents.'	Appropriate when the task is important. It is usually accompanied by a verbal, and possibly written, brief stating the task objective and how and when it should be accomplished.
Collegiate	You might say: 'We all think that this is just up your street.'	Useful when acknowledging the skills of an individual within the team, and offering them special responsibility. The whole team may have an input into the brief, which is usually verbal.
Laissez-faire	You might say: 'I'm not going to tell you how to do the job. I'll leave that up to you.'	Highly appropriate style for use with skilled and experienced staff. You rely on them to assume responsibility, make key decisions without supervision or follow-up.
Trouble-shooting	You might say: 'We have a truancy problem with some boys in Y10 that I would like you to sort out.'	You have faith in their ability to be creative in order that the problem is dealt with. Your task is to outline the problem – they will do the rest.
Right-hand	You might say: 'I've done this for the last few years. I'd like you to take it off my shoulders and improve it.'	Useful when you delegate a key task to a trusted individual whose fresh approach may provide some new impetus. You are regularly informed of progress.

HOW CAN I BUILD IN EFFECTIVE AND RESPONSIVE MONITORING AND SUPPORT?

Monitoring is crucial, but in a coaching and controlling form, rather than as interference. Failure to monitor and support, especially at the beginning, may mean that the tiniest of errors could result in a whole job being completed wrongly. In your role as team leader you are then left with having to manage that failure, sort the task out and re-motivate the individual member of staff. Effective monitoring enables you to spot the error early on and correct it before things go awry.

An effective monitoring system needs to find the right combination of 'light rein' and 'tight hand'. It needs to be done with firmness, tact and sensitivity. An important factor in determining whether to adopt a 'hands-on' or 'hands-off' approach to monitoring is the level of experience of your team member. It is probably self-evident that, if your colleague has a considerable level of experience and expertise at handling similar tasks, he or she will require less monitoring than someone with little or none. Make use of the monitoring process to provide opportunities for assessing and extending your colleague's abilities and to provide the necessary coaching and training. Delegating tasks to first-time or less experienced staff requires careful briefing and closer monitoring especially during the early stages. Take every opportunity to build their confidence by focusing on, and praising, good performance. If errors are made, coach your staff in ways of avoiding them in future. Don't be reluctant to utilize experienced team colleagues to help you monitor.

Maintaining an appropriate distance between yourself and those undertaking delegated tasks is never easy. Because others are unlikely to work in exactly the same way as you do, try to resist the temptation to intervene the minute you judge the task is not being performed 'your way'. Simply set up a system of regular checks, meetings and reports (formal or informal) to satisfy yourself that the task is on track. The progress review should fit very neatly into your school's performance management arrangements – planning, monitoring and review – so that you are not duplicating effort. Where the

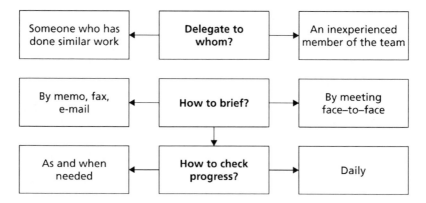

Figure 5.3 **Delegation summary chart**

review reveals difficulties or problems encountered during the delegation, it is important that the team leader identifies the causes.

Point for reflection

In the event that there has been a problem, the first step towards finding a solution is to judge whether it stems from you, the delegate, the task brief, or procedure. Consider the following self-review questions and apply them to a situation that you may have encountered.

- Should I have retained the task?
- Was I too hasty in selecting the delegate?
- Was there a better candidate?
- Could I have provided a clearer brief?
- Could I have monitored more rigorously?
- Was I accessible enough for support?
- Did I provide sufficient guidance when queries arose?
- Did the problem stem from circumstances beyond our control?
- How could I have prevented this problem from occurring?
- What would I do differently next time?
- What have I learnt about my own strengths and weaknesses?
- What have I learnt about my team colleague's strengths and weaknesses?
- Was the brief founded on the correct assumptions and facts?

WHAT PART DOES COACHING HAVE TO PLAY IN DELEGATION?

In the mind of some people coaching is restricted to situations where things have gone wrong but, such is the strength of the coaching process, it can also be used to support the delegation process. A coach, after all, helps others to perform more effectively. This could mean achieving a higher output, or completing a task in a shorter time or with less effort, or with better relationships with team members. Coaching is not telling someone how to do something, but helping them to find the best way for themselves – unlocking potential to maximize performance. (Chapter 10 is devoted to a fuller consideration of coaching.)

SUMMARY SELF-REVIEW

Spend a little time considering and then responding to the following review questions:

1. How regularly do I assign challenging tasks and projects to develop the potential of individuals within my team?

2. How appropriately do I use delegation as a motivation tool to help team members achieve desired outcomes?

3. When delegating tasks, how carefully do I consider the skills and attributes of individual team members?

4. When delegating tasks, how readily do I assign both responsibility and authority for work?

5. How clearly do I spell out the desired outcomes and performance standards required when delegating work to team members?

6. How closely do I consider an individual's interests, strengths and other work commitments when assigning tasks?

7. How effectively do I support and encourage my team members when performing delegated work?

8. When delegating a task, do I also include and discuss the necessary resources to be successful?

9. How actively do I encourage individuals to resolve their own problems by delegating authority to address issues?

10. How hesitant am I to admit that I need help to keep on top of my job?

11. How readily do I ask the team for their ideas about problems that arise in their work?

12. How available am I to staff who may want to discuss the work I have delegated to them?

13. How do I ensure that I provide positive feedback to my team?

14. How readily would I replace someone to whom I have delegated if they are not up to the task?

15. How systematically do I invite feedback from those to whom I delegate tasks?

16. How good am I at learning lessons from delegations that were not totally successful?

Action planning

Having spent some time reviewing your approach to delegation, identify some actions that you might take to strengthen your current approach.

6 Improving the Effectiveness of Team Meetings

The Law of Triviality, briefly stated, means that the time spent on any item of the agenda will be in inverse proportion to the sum involved.

(C. Northcote Parkinson, 1958)

INTRODUCTION

Meetings are commonplace in schools. With meetings taking place so frequently we might expect them to be a source of satisfaction and accomplishment. Many are, of course. However, the opposite is often the case. This chapter sets out to help team leaders improve the effectiveness of the meetings they lead and, indeed, attend. It begins with the premiss that effective meetings are ones that achieve their objectives within a reasonable time. The chapter looks at several conditions and actions that help bring about successful meetings and offers responses to the following key questions likely to be posed by team leaders:

> ➤ Why meet at all?

> ➤ What are the advantages of meetings over other forms of communication?

> ➤ Are there different kinds of meetings?

> ➤ What do we mean by an effective meeting?

> ➤ What makes meetings ineffective?

> ➤ What is a good way of achieving effective meetings?

> ➤ How important is the meeting leader's role?

> ➤ How can I encourage contributions from team members and stimulate discussion?

> ➤ How vital to the meeting is an agenda? What should I take into account when preparing an agenda?

> ➤ How important is the meeting environment?

> ➤ What can I learn from observing the contributions made by team members at meetings?

> ➤ How should I deal with problem people at meetings?

> ➤ How do I take accurate notes of decisions taken at meetings?

> ➤ How do I run a meeting using formal procedures?

WHY MEET AT ALL?

In most schools a schedule of meetings is drawn up ahead of the start of the school year to ensure that all teams are provided with sufficient time to meet. This is sometimes done on a rota basis. This system has huge advantages because teams get used to a schedule of regular meetings. The disadvantage of this approach is that it does not cater for those occasions when meetings are not needed and other times when additional meetings are needed because of uneven workloads. On occasions, team leaders should be allowed the flexibility to depart from the meetings schedule, if it can be shown that the time could be more gainfully used elsewhere. As has often been said in this book, where colleagues are trusted and valued there tends to be room for greater flexibility in relation to these matters. In general, meetings are gatherings of three or more people sharing common objectives, where face-to-face communication is the primary means of achieving those objectives. Managed well, meetings can therefore achieve and support a range of purposes. For example, they can be particularly useful for:

- identifying and solving problems;

- reaching agreement on procedures;

- defining policy;

- giving information;

- seeking information;

- motivating people and generating commitment;

- resolving conflicts;

- ensuring clear communication between team leaders and team members, and between team members;

- gathering ideas from team members;

- clarifying matters and intentions;

- improving decision-making skills among team members; and

- providing a sense of involvement.

Point for reflection

Meetings cost time and money, both of which are valuable. Consider the last two meetings you attended in terms of their worth and necessity, against the following criteria:

- Did I give up anything to attend?
- What decisions were taken?
- Did I have a choice whether to attend or not? If so, why did I?
- What did I contribute to (a) discussion, (b) decision-making?
- If I did neither, why was I there?

- Have the decisions of the meeting been implemented?
- Would the outcome have happened anyway, even without the meeting?
- Could I have spent my time more productively elsewhere?
- Have I any idea of the cost of the meeting? Try to work it out using:
  Cost of time of those present
  Cost of cover for those present   =
  Accommodation cost   =
  Cost of time spent preparing and following up =
  TOTAL COST   =

What conclusions do you draw from this activity?

WHAT ARE THE ADVANTAGES OF MEETINGS OVER OTHER FORMS OF COMMUNICATION?

Understandably, and perhaps inevitably, meetings get a mixed press. Despite being time-consuming, meetings are, nonetheless, essential to the effective operation of teams and a way of achieving team objectives. Even those who use video-conferencing agree that it is only ever second best to actually meeting with people face to face. However, team leaders need to be clear about the purpose of meetings and their preferred outcomes. Such considerations will determine, among other things, who should be present, and how much time should be allocated in total as well as to individual agenda items. Some of the advantages of holding meetings over other forms of communication include the following:

- everyone gets the same message at the same time;

- it is possible to assess people's reactions and understanding;

- queries and problems are resolved on the spot;

- there is encouragement to work as a team;

- meetings can create a sense of belonging and joint responsibility; and

- meetings help each member of the team to understand the collective aim of the group and the way in which their own work can contribute to the team's success.

ARE THERE DIFFERENT KINDS OF MEETINGS?

Generally speaking, meetings can be grouped into two major categories, with each category having two components:

- **Information meetings**
  - advising/updating
  - selling

- Decision-making meetings
  - goal setting
  - problem-solving

This classification is helpful because each type of meeting requires team leaders to conduct them differently. To be effective, those leading and attending meetings need to understand their purpose. The Table 6.1 summarizes some considerations for team leaders as they plan for the two kinds of meetings.

Table 6.1 Planning considerations for the two main meeting types

Important considerations	Information meetings	Decision-making meetings
How many should attend?	Any number, e.g. whole staff	Preferably not more than ten
Who should attend?	Those who need to know the information being given	Those responsible and those who can contribute
What communication process is best?	One-way from team leader to participants with opportunities for questions	Interactive discussion among all attending
How should the room be arranged?	Participants facing front of room – classroom style	Participants facing each other – conference style/ informal
What is the most effective style of leadership?	Authoritative	Participative
What should be emphasized?	Content	Interaction and problem-solving
What is the key to success?	Planning and preparation of information to be presented	Meeting climate that supports open, free expression

WHAT DO WE MEAN BY AN EFFECTIVE MEETING?

Effective meetings are those where the outcomes are met to the satisfaction of those present, in the time allocated (or sooner!). It is possible to judge the effectiveness of a meeting by asking the following questions:

- Did the *outcomes* of the meeting justify the time spent on it?
- Could the *outcomes* have been better?
- How will the *outcomes* be acted upon?

Point for reflection
Try applying the above 'criteria' by considering one or more typical meetings you attend. Compare your meeting(s) to the following characteristics of effective meetings and tick those characteristics present.

1   An agenda is prepared.
2   Meeting participants have an opportunity to contribute to the agenda.
3   Advance notice of meeting time and place is provided to those invited.
4   Meeting facilities are comfortable and adequate for the number of participants.
5   The meeting begins on time.
6   The meeting has a scheduled ending time.
7   The use of time is monitored throughout the meeting.
8   Everyone has an opportunity to present their point of view.
9   Participants listen attentively to each other.
10   There are periodic summaries as the meeting progresses.
11   No one tends to dominate the discussion.
12   Everyone has a voice in decisions made at the meeting.
13   The meeting typically ends with a summary of decisions and accomplishments.
14   The meeting is periodically evaluated by participants.
15   People can be depended upon to carry out any action agreed to during the meeting.
16   A note of discussion or minutes of the meeting is provided to each participant following the meeting.
17   The leader of the meeting follows up with participants on action agreed to during the meeting.
18   The appropriate and necessary people can be counted on to attend each meeting.
19   The decision process used is appropriate for the size of the group.
20   When used, audio-visual equipment is in good working condition and does not detract from the meeting.

WHAT MAKES MEETINGS INEFFECTIVE?

It follows that if certain factors facilitate more effective meetings, there are other factors that achieve the opposite effect. Meetings often fail to meet their achievement targets and, as a result, become time-wasters because some or all of the following factors are present:

- the meeting's purpose is not stated clearly;
- the wrong participants attend the meeting;
- too many meetings are held;
- poor or no minutes are published;
- irrelevant talk takes place within the meeting;
- no conclusions are drawn at the meeting;
- no follow-up to the meeting takes place;

- indecision means that the meeting achieves nothing;

- the meeting fails to start on time;

- too many interruptions occur during the meeting;

- people go off in different directions at the same time;

- the chairperson does not stick to the agenda;

- people find it difficult to participate;

- too much information is given at one time;

- hidden agendas;

- lack of commitment from team members;

- the agenda is boring or uninspiring;

- people do not listen to what is said – preferring to hear what they want to hear;

- poor environment – making hearing difficult, room too hot or too cold, room too crowded;

- lack of openness and trust;

- poor preparation on the part of the person chairing the meeting; and

- the meeting goes on too long.

Organizing successful meetings is demanding and team leaders should give considerable thought to ways of making meetings productive and functional. Remember:

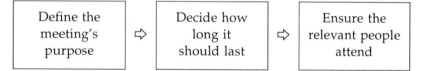

| Define the meeting's purpose | ⇨ | Decide how long it should last | ⇨ | Ensure the relevant people attend |

WHAT IS A GOOD WAY OF ACHIEVING EFFECTIVE MEETINGS?

In brief, this can only be achieved by minimizing or, better still, eliminating the factors listed in the previous section. A great deal can be done to improve the chances of meetings being more productive by adopting a five-step plan, as shown in Table 6.2.

HOW IMPORTANT IS THE MEETING LEADER'S ROLE?

The meeting leader must focus the energy and attention of those attending and keep them moving toward the meeting's objectives. This is an important

Table 6.2 **A five-step plan for achieving effective meetings**

Step	What to do
Step 1: Plan	Plan the objectives of the meeting in advance, and be clear about what the meeting is intended to achieve. Plan the meeting by deciding: • Who should attend? • What is the purpose of the meeting? • Where and when will it be held? • How long should the meeting be? • What time will the meeting start and finish? • What items will be on the agenda? • How should the agenda items be ordered? • How much time should be spent on each agenda item? • What supporting papers are needed? • What facilities and equipment are required? • How should the meeting room be arranged?
Step 2: Inform	Keep other members of the meeting informed about: • what is to be discussed; • why it is being discussed; • what needs to be achieved following the discussion. Arrange for the most appropriate people and the correct information to be there and for supporting papers to be issued in advance.
Step 3: Prepare	Arrange an agenda in its proper sequence and allot the correct amount of time for each subject. Bear in mind the consequences of allowing those items that are urgent to take up more time than those which are important.
Step 4: Structure	Structure the discussion in stages so that all the data and facts come before any interpretations are made, and all the interpretation before a decision on the action. Keep the stages separate. Stop people jumping on or going back over old ground. In summary: • set a business-like tone by starting on time; • adopt a relaxed and collegiate team ethos; • clearly define roles within the meeting; • agree the arrangements for making notes of decisions made; • keep to time; • keep people on task; • ensure action points are clear.
Step 5: Summarize and record	• summarize and record decisions and action points; • remind team members of action points agreed upon; • set the date and time of the next meeting; • evaluate the meeting; • close the meeting positively and with thanks; • monitor action points.

multifaceted task for the meeting leader who has to monitor progress and provide direction. If we look at the role in more detail, it requires the meeting leader to be attentive to each of the following meeting components:

• **Content** – the knowledge, experience, opinions, ideas, myths, attitudes, and expectations of those attending.

- **Interaction** – the way attendees work together while processing the meeting's content; involves feelings, attitudes, cooperation, trust, participation and openness.

- **Structure** – the way in which both the information and participants are organized to achieve the meeting's purpose.

Point for reflection

Evaluate the next meeting you conduct and try to identify the activities you performed in your attempt to be attentive to the three components mentioned above – content, interaction and structure. Some of these activities are included for you.

- Content
  - *keeping on track*
  - *summarizing*
- Interaction
  - *monitoring participation*
  - *encouraging participation*
- Structure
  - *developing an agenda*
  - *managing time*

HOW CAN I ENCOURAGE CONTRIBUTIONS FROM TEAM MEMBERS AND STIMULATE DISCUSSION?

The success of most meetings depends upon appropriate participation from all parties. A climate of open exchange will only be created when those attending recognize that a mutual sharing of views and ideas is valued. As shown in Table 6.3, the skilful use of questioning will normally encourage contributions and discussion.

HOW VITAL TO THE MEETING IS AN AGENDA? WHAT SHOULD I TAKE INTO ACCOUNT WHEN PREPARING AN AGENDA?

Every meeting should have an agenda and, if at all possible, this should be given in advance to each participant. Without an agenda, gaining any form of control is very difficult. A properly drawn up agenda informs those attending the meeting what the meeting is about, how long each item is going to take and what their contribution is expected to be. It follows, then, that team members need to know in advance so that they can prepare their contributions, at least mentally. In summary, the agenda should provide the following information:

- confirmation of the date of the meeting;
- the start and finishing time of the meeting;

Table 6.3 Encouraging contributions and stimulating discussion at meetings

Things you could try	Sample questions
Asking for feelings and opinions	• *Pete, what is your reaction to . . .?* • *What is your thinking on . . ., Judy?* • *What prompted your decision to . . ., Andy?*
Paraphrasing	• *Let me see whether I understand your point.* • *Before we go on, am I right in thinking . . .?* • *I'm not sure whether I understand, are you suggesting that we should . . .?*
Encouraging participation	• *Jane, how do you feel about this?* • *Derek, how would you respond to Maria's question?* • *Before we go on, I'd like to hear from Maureen on this.*
Asking for a summary	• *We've heard some great ideas. Tony, would you summarize for us please?* • *I've lost track, will someone summarize what we've agreed, please?*
Asking for clarification	• *I'm still not clear. What do I do when . . .?* • *What happens if . . .? Can someone clarify that for me?*
Asking for examples	• *Dot, could you give us an example of that?* • *Belinda, can you expand on that? I'm not sure that I understood all of it.*
Checking for consensus	• *It seems to me that there is some agreement here. Does everyone accept this proposal?* • *Brian, is that your feeling too?*
Prompting action	• *How do you think we should . . .?* • *Francis, how do you think we should proceed now?*
Exploring matters in more detail	• *What other ways are there of dealing with this?* • *Are there other things we should consider?*
Suggesting action	• *I notice that Gordon has done most of the talking on this issue. It may be sensible if you were to prepare some recommendations in time for our next meeting, Gordon.*
Sharing feelings	• *I feel that you are not giving Kate a chance to explain her position.* • *I'm getting confused. I think we should take this issue up next week when we meet. How do the rest of you feel?*
Reflecting what someone else is feeling	• *Cathy, I get the impression that you are not happy with my reasoning. Is that right?* • *Keith's comments tell me that he needs to ask some questions on this. Is that right, Keith?*
Being supportive	• *Let's give Tony a chance to tell it the way he sees it.* • *Pat, you've had your say. Now it's Sam's turn. Give her a chance to explain.*
Questioning assumptions	• *What you suggest assumes that, unless we change the date, they won't attend. Is that right?* • *Your proposal assumes that we cannot increase attendance in Year 11. Is that right?*
Confronting differences	• *Nicky, you haven't said much but you don't appear to agree. Is that right?* • *Liz, you seem to be holding back on this. Is there something you disagree with?*

Table 6.3 *Continued*

Things you could try	Sample questions
Reversing roles	• *Why don't we look at it from the student's point of view, for a minute. How would we react?* • *Pretend that you are a new parent at the school. What do you think they would say?*
Looking into the future	• *If we went ahead, what's the worse case scenario?* • *If it doesn't work, what have we lost?*
Focusing on action choice	• *Well, I think we've looked at it from all sides, so let's choose from our alternatives.* • *We've discussed both points of view. It's time we made a choice.*

- the venue for the meeting;

- those expected to attend;

- the period of time to be spent on each item on the agenda; and

- the content of each item, plus expected actions, outcomes, and decisions.

An example agenda is shown in Figure 6.1.

Agenda
Senior Management Team Meeting

From: Dave

Date: 14th May

Time: 3.45–5.00 (at the latest)

Venue: Room 11

Attendees: Brian, Debbie, Frankie, Linda, Sam, Tom (scribe)

Time allocation	Subject	Main responsibility
5 minutes	Feedback from last week's parents' evening – what do we need to change, if anything?	Dave
10 minutes	HEI Initial Teacher Training – student placements – agreeing arrangements	Frankie
10 minutes	Refurbishment of resources area – when? How?	Sam
30 minutes	Revisions to the performance management policy – identify, discuss and approve changes	Dave and Linda
10 minutes	CPD for next year – team use of closure days	Brian
10 minutes	Summary and reminder of action needed	Dave

Figure 6.1 **Example agenda**

Point for reflection

Think of a meeting you are due to lead in the near future. Consider the items that need to be discussed and the sequence in which they should be handled. Estimate the time required for each item. From this estimate, set a probable ending time.

HOW IMPORTANT IS THE MEETING ENVIRONMENT?

It is essential not to underestimate the importance of matters such as the environment, facilities, refreshments and seating arrangements. Ensure that these kinds of arrangements are in place and fit for purpose because they will have an influence on the effectiveness of the meeting. For example, the provision of refreshments is always appreciated by colleagues and helps to set a relaxed tone – it even encourages punctuality! The need for those attending to be physically comfortable should not be overlooked. Also, heating/cooling, lighting and ventilation should be adequate for the size of the meeting.

Strange as it may seem, the arrangement of chairs and tables and the placement of attendees in a meeting can also have an influence on the success of meetings. Be guided by the communication needs for the type of meeting you plan to hold. For example, is it important for colleagues to maintain eye contact, or is the meeting a presentation thus requiring attendees to face the front of the room? The significance of seating positions depends on where the team leader or chair sits. Decide what you want from the meeting, and arrange the seating to help you achieve this. For controversial issues, you may wish to split up factions and avoid seating people who hold opposing views next to each other. Don't forget that eye contact is crucial in communicating to team members what steps you want to take next. Ask yourself who should be able to make eye contact with whom, and encourage people to sit accordingly. Below are a few examples of seating arrangements together with some considerations on their use:

- **Circular** – An arrangement of chairs around a circular table can:
  - provide a sense of togetherness;
  - encourage eye contact;
  - discourage 'power' seats i.e. everyone is equal;
  - be useful for encouraging informal discussions; and
  - heighten moods e.g. aggression.
- **Rectangular** – An arrangement of chairs around a rectangular table can:
  - encourage people to take sides and to sit opposite those whom they wish to confront;
  - encourage the chair to sit at the head of the table reinforcing the sense of hierarchy; and

- encourage the chair to sit in the centre of one side, thus reinforcing neutrality.

- **Semi-circular** – A semi-circular arrangement of chairs (with or without tables) can:

  - encourage participants to face the question written on a flip chart as well as the facilitator or chair; and

  - help focus the energy of the group towards a common problem – this arrangement is ideal for presentations and problem–solving sessions.

WHAT CAN I LEARN FROM OBSERVING THE CONTRIBUTIONS MADE BY TEAM MEMBERS AT MEETINGS?

As well as being aware of the purpose of meetings, it is also important to understand the way they work. By this I mean, what is actually happening, where the contributions are coming from (and, perhaps significantly, where they might *not* be coming from) and how frequently, who is being deliberately obstructive or evasive. Being effective in leading a meeting requires you to recognize what people are feeling during it. Body language is often a giveaway. Participants' reaction needs to be acknowledged and brought out into the open. There is a balance to be struck between getting meetings over more quickly and developing a process that provides participants with support and encouragement that make meetings worthwhile. Handling the diversity of responses in meetings requires sensitivity to the group process that is going on. Table 6.4 may help you analyse the nature of the interaction taking place among team members.

Point for reflection

At a future meeting, observe a range of your team members' body language. Try to observe the following:

- How people sit.
- Their facial expressions.
- How people use smiles and nods.
- How people use their hands, wrists, fingers.
- How people use eye contact.

What other kinds of body language can you see?

HOW SHOULD I DEAL WITH PROBLEM PEOPLE AT MEETINGS?

Occasionally, meetings have been known to bring out the very worst behaviour from team members (and team leaders!). The interpersonal skills of the team leader, coupled with effective chairing, resolve many of these problems but, at times, strategies are required in order to deal with team members who display some of the following negative behaviours:

Table 6.4   Team member interactions at meetings

Nature of interaction	Characteristic behaviours	Examples
Proposing	Putting forward a new suggestion, proposal, or course of action.	'Let's ask Mat to look into that. He's up to date.' 'I suggest that we review this before the end of May.'
Building	Proposing action that extends or develops a suggestion made by another team member.	'. . . and your plan would be even better if we added a second reporting stage.' 'I like Jo's idea. Why don't we also involve the governors.'
Supporting	Direct declaration of agreement or support for another team member.	'Yes, I go along with that.' 'Sounds fine to me.'
Disagreeing	Direct disagreement or objection to another team member's ideas or suggestions.	'No, I don't agree with that.' 'I don't like that idea at all. It just won't work.'
Defending/attacking	Attacking another person either directly or defensively.	'That's stupid.' '. . . and your third point is either incompetence or a lie.'
Testing understanding	Attempting to establish whether or not an earlier contribution has been understood.	'Can I just check that we're talking about the same thing here?' 'Can I take it that we are all agreed on this?'
Summarizing	Summarizing or restating, in a concise way, the substance of previous discussions or events.	'So far, then we have agreed to revise the assessment policy by the end of March and issue a draft to staff for consultation by the middle of April.'
Seeking information	Seeking facts, opinions, or clarification from another team member.	'Can anyone tell me how other schools deal with this kind of thing?' 'Have you checked the situation in the last day or two?'
Giving information	Offering facts, opinions, or clarification to the team.	'I know of a school that dealt with this kind of incident very successfully last year.' 'There have been at least three incidents today.'
Involving	Direct attempts to involve others or to increase their opportunity to contribute	'Sarah, what do you think?' 'Dave, how do feel about what is being suggested?'
Excluding	Shutting out others or reducing their opportunity to contribute, e.g. by interrupting	'I suggest that only those of us who have been around for some time can really comment on this.' 'Just a minute, Jen.'

- arriving late and causing some disruption to the flow of the meeting;
- leaving early and causing some disruption to the flow of the meeting;
- insisting on answering telephone calls;
- responding negatively to everyone's suggestions;
- using non-verbal communication to express disagreement, boredom, frustration, etc.;
- engaging in alternative activity, e.g. marking, reading material unconnected with the topic under consideration;
- constantly whispering to a neighbour;
- using status, qualifications, length of service to argue a point;
- talking too much and dominating the meeting;
- introducing irrelevancies; and
- launching personal attacks on other team members.

Table 6.5 outlines certain behaviours shown by those attending meetings and ways in which team leaders might deal with the situations successfully.

Remember:

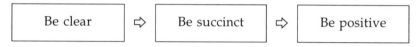

Point for reflection
Table 6.6 lists some situations that may confront you when leading a team meeting. Consider each situation in turn and select your preferred solution from the options on offer.

HOW DO I TAKE ACCURATE NOTES OF DECISIONS TAKEN AT MEETINGS?

Notes (or minutes) taken at meetings need to reflect actions and decisions taken or to be taken. As a general rule, notes of meetings should record:

- the date and time of the meeting;
- where it was held;
- who chaired the meeting and the names of all present, together with apologies for absence;
- all agenda items discussed and decisions reached;
- the name of the person responsible for the action in each case;

Table 6.5 **Some strategies for dealing with problem people in meetings**

Situations/behaviours	How to handle them
Silent and shy team members	These are colleagues who can be painfully shy but often have a lot to offer the team. Try to make them feel as comfortable as possible during your meeting. Start by asking them simple questions and make eye contact with them as they answer to let them know that their input is valued. Recognize contributions immediately and sincerely and encourage more.
Dominant, pompous and self-opinionated team members	They think they know everything and often manipulate every conversation and seek control. Sometimes they have great insights to share but choose not to. If confronted directly in meetings, they will only seek more control and become overbearing. Because they love to share their knowledge, try to seek their advice prior to the meeting. They will love providing their expertise and perhaps won't need to dominate the meeting discussion later. Also, try to establish a meeting procedure that affords equal time to others so that you don't have to ask these colleagues to back off during the meeting.
Argumentative, antagonistic or sceptical team members	Argumentative members of the team question everything, criticize ideas and even attack others personally. They want attention and can't get it through other means, so they always take on the role of devil's advocate. They see problems but seldom volunteer solutions. To discourage negative behaviour, try early on to give them the attention they require. Invite ideas instead of allowing them to judge and criticize everyone else's.
Team members who seem distracted and distract others	These characters like to show their disinterest in meetings. They engage in side discussions, read other materials and generally attempt to remain uninvolved. Basically, these team members crave attention so ask them to share their opinions of the discussion at hand. In this way, at least they are focused on the meeting issues and not on social interaction.
Indifferent team members	They never speak up in meetings because they cannot be bothered. They are easygoing and generally make a point of always going with the flow. They don't get involved in meeting discussions or offer help or support to others. Meetings make them yawn – they require too much effort to get involved. To get them involved and interested, ask them to plan and lead future meetings.
Team members who start another meeting with neighbours	The problem is more likely to arise in a larger group. It may be the result of the need to speak when unable to address the group as a whole, or it may be the result of a more cautious thinker's desire to try out an idea before sharing it with the group. Side conversations are not really a problem unless they become prolonged. Try inviting the individual to share with everyone what is being said. Another way to handle this situation is to simply be quiet and look at the offending team member.

Table 6.6 Confronting difficult situations

Your situation	What do you do?
You arrive a little early for your team meeting to find that the meeting room is arranged differently from the way you would like it.	<ul><li>Rearrange the room yourself.</li><li>Wait until your team members begin to arrive and have them rearrange things.</li><li>Contact the site manager and ask for it to be rearranged.</li><li>Cancel the meeting.</li></ul>
You are expecting your team of eight participants for a 1000 meeting. It is now 1005 and only six have arrived. No one has advised you of plans to arrive late.	<ul><li>Start the meeting with those present.</li><li>Telephone the two absent colleagues to see if they are coming.</li><li>Wait another five minutes and then begin.</li><li>Ask those present whether they would like to begin now or later.</li></ul>
You want discussion on a topic but no one is talking.	<ul><li>Ask a general question of the team.</li><li>Ask a specific question of an individual.</li><li>Ask for feedback on why no one is talking.</li><li>End the meeting due to lack of interest.</li></ul>
You notice, through non-verbal cues, that the interest level of the team is fading.	<ul><li>Shorten the agenda and end the meeting.</li><li>Take a short break.</li><li>Speak in a more animated fashion.</li><li>Try to start a discussion.</li></ul>
One of your team is using too much time talking about an item that is not on the agenda.	<ul><li>Interrupt, stressing the need to return to the agenda.</li><li>Ignore it and hope that the meeting makes some progress.</li><li>Ask the team if they want to discuss the subject.</li><li>Tell the team member that the item will be taken up at the end of the meeting.</li></ul>
The team is getting away from the purpose of the meeting.	<ul><li>Let things go as long as everyone seems interested.</li><li>Interrupt and refer the team back to the agenda.</li><li>Gain a view from the team on whether or not to continue this discussion.</li><li>Take a break to allow the discussion to continue outside the meeting.</li></ul>
Two people, sitting together, keep whispering to each other. It has been going on for some time. You find it distracting.	<ul><li>Ask them to share their discussion with the rest of the team.</li><li>Stop talking and look at them.</li><li>Ignore it and hope they finish soon.</li><li>Ask them a specific question to see if they were listening.</li></ul>

- any significant points raised in discussion;

- the time at which the meeting ended; and

- the date, time and location of the next meeting.

Minutes should be action documents and therefore should not attempt to record:

- every single word that was uttered;

- everyone that contributed;

- all the alternative viewpoints; and

- verbatim comments.

Point for reflection

Now that you are more aware of what notes of meetings should contain, comment on the style and formats used by staff at your school e.g. senior staff, governors, departments, etc. Are there particularly good examples that you could adopt or adapt?

HOW DO I RUN A MEETING USING FORMAL PROCEDURES?

Even if as a team leader you are not required to lead meetings using formal procedures, you will often be expected or required to attend meetings that do use such procedures, e.g. meetings of governors, sub-committees, etc. Table 6.7 will help you to understand the format of such meetings. Running meetings using formal procedures provides a pre-prepared framework. You can make good use of established procedures to help meetings run smoothly and achieve their objectives.

Figure 6.2 summarizes the process of managing meetings.

Table 6.7 **Running meetings according to formal procedures**

Stage in procedure	Comments and guidance
Meeting formally opened	Even before the formal start of the meeting, the person chairing the meeting should ensure that the following conditions have been met: • all those required to attend have been given proper notice; • a quorum of people is present; • a register of attendees is kept. If any of the conditions are not met, the meeting may be adjourned or, if appropriate, delayed. Once the criteria are met, begin the meeting by calling for everyone's attention, making the necessary formal introductions, e.g. newcomers, those attending to provide input to specific items on the agenda.
Previous minutes approved	Gaining approval for the minutes of the previous meeting is an early and, generally, not too time-consuming task at a regular formal meeting. The chair should ensure that everyone agrees that decisions have been recorded accurately. This is usually achieved by inviting a show of hands from those who are eligible. Remember that the minutes form the official record of events at meetings.
Routine business dealt with	Part of the chair's responsibility is to deal with routine matters, e.g. reports from sub-committees. Raise each routine matter and elicit the approval of the attendees before moving on to the next. Record decisions for inclusion in the minutes
Motions proposed	In formal meetings, non-routine matters on the agenda are dealt with through proposed motions – clear statements showing a wish to do something
Meeting closed	

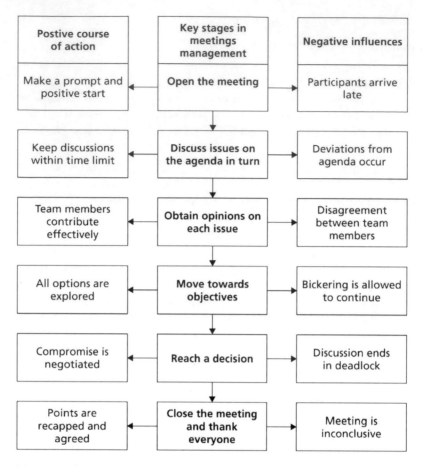

Figure 6.2 **Managing meetings summary chart**

SUMMARY SELF-REVIEW

Spend a little time considering and then responding to the following review questions:

1. How clear are my objectives for the meetings I hold?

2. How selective am I about inviting participants?

3. How well do I prepare the agenda?

4. How far in advance of the meeting is it usually distributed?

5. Do I arrive early enough to check the arrangements?

6. How confident am I about starting the meeting promptly regardless of who is present?

7. How successfully do I follow the agenda?

8. How successfully do I manage time and conclude the meeting as scheduled?

9. How effective am I at eliciting everyone's participation?

10. How successfully do I help in the resolution of any conflicts that may arise in meetings?

11. How well do I maintain proper control of the discussion?

12. How effectively do I summarize accomplishments at the end of the meeting and clarify any action to be taken?

13. Do I prepare and distribute notes of the meeting/record of discussions and decisions?

14. Do I request evaluative feedback from participants?

15. How well do I take agreed-upon action?

16. How effectively do I follow up on action to be taken by others?

Action planning

Having spent some time reviewing your approach to managing meetings, identify some actions that you might take to strengthen your current approach.

7 Handling Conflict Situations Successfully

Why is there no conflict at this meeting? Something's wrong when there's no conflict.

(Michael Eisner, Disney chief)

INTRODUCTION

Conflict at work needs to be kept in perspective. In schools, team leaders rarely work in isolation and, as in most organizations, there are rules and agreed ways of doing things – some formal, others less so. The teams we lead, and often inherit, usually have an established set of ground rules. We quickly come to understand 'the way things are done around here'. Part of this agreed code of behaviour will involve managing conflict resolution. Our personal attitude towards conflict will significantly influence the way conflict is viewed and utilized. This chapter explains what is meant by conflict, how it arises and how it manifests itself. By responding to the following questions likely to be posed by team leaders, the chapter also offers common-sense guidance on how you might use conflict in a positive way to channel the energies of your team members:

➢ What do we mean by conflict?

➢ What are the key ingredients of conflict?

➢ What are the possible causes of conflict?

➢ How might I deal with any conflict that could arise within the team?

➢ Is there an ideal conflict resolution style?

➢ Is conflict always negative? Can conflict ever be constructive?

➢ What if all else fails and conflict continues?

➢ What coping strategies should I employ to deal with a difficult team member who refuses to perform?

➢ But, if there simply is no warning, how do I take the heat out of a conflict situation?

WHAT DO WE MEAN BY CONFLICT?

Conflict is a natural disagreement resulting from individuals or groups that differ in attitudes, beliefs, values or needs. Some would say that conflict is a natural event that forms part of nearly every working day. After all, conflict starts off as nothing more than highly determined action to achieve a preferred outcome. This in itself need not be a problem. What makes it problematic is that having secured the outcome, it precludes others from achieving their preferred outcome – and that is where hostility raises its head. It is the hostility that is usually seen as the harmful aspect of conflict. It becomes an even greater problem if the hostility is handled badly or is allowed to continue for so long that it destroys team working. Conflict also comes in a variety of forms:

- **Goal conflict** – when one person or one group of people seeks a different outcome from another.

- **Cognitive conflict** – when a person or a group hold ideas that conflict with those held by others.

- **Affective conflict** – where one person's or group's emotions, feelings or attitudes are incompatible with others'.

- **Behavioural conflict** – where one person or group behaves in a way that others find unacceptable.

Conflict manifests itself through a variety of behaviours, ranging from mute disagreement to public anger. You are likely to recognize the hostility and rage associated with conflict – a person with a flushed complexion, who is breathing shallowly, sweating, clenching their fist, speaking quickly and sometimes incoherently. We may think of these as disproportionate ways of reacting to events – but it is *their* way. People in conflict can also be quiet and withdrawn – they just don't show what they feel so obviously. Only by getting to know your team members as individuals can you recognize their reactions and try to pre-empt potential conflict situations.

Point for reflection

How do you typically respond when you seriously disagree with someone? Do you

- **get mad inside but keep quiet and give the other the 'silent' treatment?**
- **withdraw to a safe distance because you don't like to argue?**
- **get angry, criticize, call names, use sarcasm or some other aggressive behaviour?**
- **give in; say 'I guess you are right' with a big sigh; be submissive in order to avoid conflict?**
- **deny or pretend that 'everything is okay' – no conflict exists?**

These are quite common methods for coping with conflict. How successful or unsuccessful would you judge these to be?

WHAT ARE THE KEY INGREDIENTS OF CONFLICT?

Conflict has certain key ingredients that characterize its form and impact on the work of teams. These are described in Table 7.1.

Table 7.1 The key ingredients of conflict

Ingredient	How conflict can arise
Team needs	Team needs are things that are essential to the well-being of that team. Conflicts arise when these needs are ignored. It is important not to confuse needs with desires (things we would like, but that are not essential).
Team perceptions	People interpret reality in different ways. They perceive differences in the severity, causes and consequences of problems. Differing perceptions may come from self-perceptions, others' perceptions, conflicting perceptions of situations, and perceptions of threat.
Team power	How people use and define power is an important influence on the number and types of conflicts that occur. This also influences how conflict is managed. Conflicts can arise when people try to make others change their actions to gain an unfair advantage.
Team values	Values are beliefs or principles we consider to be very important. Serious conflicts arise when people hold incompatible values or when values are not clear. Conflicts also arise when one party refuses to accept the fact that others hold something as a value rather than a preference.
Team feelings and emotions	Many people let their feelings and emotions become a major influence over how they deal with conflict. Conflicts can also occur because people ignore their own or others' feelings and emotions.

WHAT ARE THE POSSIBLE CAUSES OF CONFLICT?

Human behaviour studies (e.g. Armstrong, 1994) show that some conflict is inevitable in human relationships (Figure 7.1). Often conflicts are the result of perceived differences rather than real ones.

Specific problems or issues

These can be both simple and complex in their nature. At their simplest, they are merely misunderstandings that can be corrected very easily. At their more complex, they could stem from deeply held views upon which a team member may be unprepared to concede ground.

Personal antagonism

Personality clashes and antagonism towards an individual are not unheard of within teams. Indeed, there may also be a history of conflict within your team that precedes your appointment.

Defensiveness

Conflict often causes people to be defensive; they will try to protect whatever is important to them. Few of us would like to think that someone is trying to 'get one over' on us.

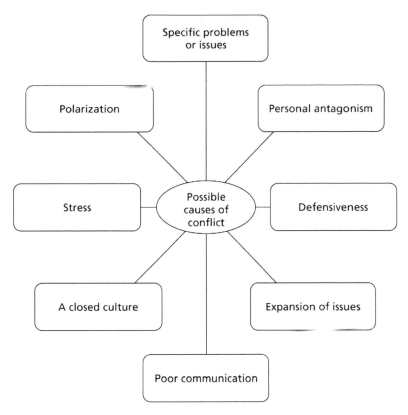

Figure 7.1 **Possible cause of conflict**

Expansion of issues

At times, team members will use conflict situations to clear the air about other, often unrelated, issues simply because they have the opportunity, e.g. '. . . and another thing . . .' As they expand the issues, they might extend the number participating in the conflict and draw them in to take sides. Team leaders would be wise to try to take the instigator to one side, to a private area in order to deal with the fundamental issues – not those that have arisen subsequently.

Poor communication

To some extent, all conflict is the product of poor communication. Team leaders need to take extra care to communicate effectively, even though it does take time. Yet, despite being time-consuming, planning how to get messages across is vital. When team members' understanding of issues is unclear they often feel insecure, and that can lead to conflict. Team members could make use of team briefings to help minimize some of the communication break-downs. Regular, but short, team briefings can help to keep the team informed of priorities, progress and policies; dispel rumours and muffle the grapevine. This free movement of information helps create a more open culture.

A closed culture

In closed cultures – ones in which there can be an over-reliance upon 'command and control' – people can often feel threatened which, in turn, can lead to an increased risk of conflict. Whenever possible, it is in team leaders' interests to offer their team colleagues some measure of control over the way they work, their work environment, etc.

Stress

Conflict and stress go hand in hand. Stress is generally the outcome of excessive pressure and this can manifest itself in conflict. The pressures at work that provoke stress and conflict are:

- the workplace – the working environment and physical conditions;

- the nature of the job – workload, involvement in decisions;

- travel – commuting difficulties;

- roles – responsibilities, boundaries;

- career – ambitions and expectations;

- relationships – both working and personal;

- individuals – personal standards, ability to cope with change; and

- work–life balance – more accurately, the 'imbalance'.

Polarization

Teams, particularly at an early stage in their maturity, may well fragment. Team members will seek support from others in the team to help them press their case or oppose change. Team leaders should stand back and gauge the situation before taking any action.

Point for reflection

Looking objectively and dispassionately at the work, attitudes and behaviours of the team, which of the above factors have been, or are most likely to be, possible causes of conflict? What steps have you/might you take to minimize the chances of conflict occurring?

HOW MIGHT I DEAL WITH ANY CONFLICT THAT COULD ARISE WITHIN THE TEAM?

It has already been stated that conflict is an inevitable, some would say vital, part of team development. Handling conflict is partially about avoiding the 'conditions' that foster conflict and partially about managing (eliminating or minimizing) the hostility that conflict seems to provoke (Figure 7.2).

PREVENTION   CONFLICT   MANAGEMENT

Figure 7.2 balancing the prevention and management of conflict

Before trying to deal with a conflict with another person in order to achieve a more positive outcome, there are five questions that need to be asked:

- Is the conflict issue really worth the effort to resolve it?
- Is the other person in the conflict really important to me?
- Will discussing the issue really improve our relationship?
- Am I willing to spend the required time and energy talking about the issue and helping the other person by listening?
- Have I chosen an appropriate time and place for the discussion to take place?

If the answer to each of these questions is 'yes', then it would seem sensible to proceed. If some answers are 'no', you may need to choose a different method of expressing your concerns, e.g. sharing feelings only, without problem-solving. You will remember from Chapter 2 that teams go through an interesting evolutionary process involving four main stages – forming, storming, norming and performing. Table 7.2 is a reminder of the four stages.

Table 7.2 **The four stages of team development (based on Tuckman, 1965)**

Stage	Stage characteristics
Forming	This is the stage when the team first gets together. Here team members are exploring each other's behaviour. There will be a lot of boundary testing – how far can we go? There is rarely any serious conflict at this stage – people tend to be well behaved, polite and tolerant. Most will keep their feelings in check just in case they overstep the boundary.
Storming	This is the most difficult stage in team development and the one where conflict is most likely to appear. Because team members are becoming familiar with one another, it is easier to express disagreement. Power and internal workings come into play and individuals will start to flex their muscles to try to impress each other by showing what they know, who they know, etc.
Norming	The team begins to settle down and team members will try to avoid conflict in an effort to achieve harmony and maintain the status quo. There is also a firmer focus on securing desired outcomes.
Performing	The team achieves much of what it decides to implement. Individuals understand and, more importantly, accept how others think and feel about contentious issues and will work positively to resolve situations. The team is happy, successful and conflict is dealt with positively.

It is quite easy to see that there is more than enough opportunity for conflict to materialize as team members attempt to deal with some or all of the following:

- individuals with different agendas;

- unclear team and/or individual objectives;

- lack of trust between team members;

- insufficient time for discussing issues;

- individuals jostling for position;

- vague team roles;

- power struggles within the team;

- disagreements about how things should be approached;

- the inflexibility of others within the team;

- lack of creativity on the part of team members;

- inward-looking tendencies;

- reluctance to leave the past and move on; and

- fear of change.

IS THERE AN IDEAL CONFLICT RESOLUTION STYLE?

Different people have different conflict resolution styles. Such styles are generally learned, often in childhood, and can appear to be automatic responses to given situations. As we assume team leader positions and encounter a range of contexts, situations and personalities, we may find that our 'preferred' style is too rigid and does not provide us with the flexibility of approach that is called for. As Figure 7.3 shows, our conflict resolution style will be dependent upon the importance we attach to:

- satisfying our personal goals; and

- sustaining particular relationships.

So, faced with a conflict situation, what styles and strategies are available to you? Table 7.3 sets out the five most common ones and the possible positive and negative impact of each on team members.

Point for reflection

Use this opportunity to analyse your conflict resolution style. Think of a situation where you, or someone you know, dealt with conflict well. Rather than focusing on the detail of the conflict itself, focus on the person dealing with the situation.

- Are you able to identify any of the styles being used?
- Describe the language and tone of the style. What precise words or phrases were being used?
- Describe the body language being used.

- Where was the situation dealt with? Was this important in resolving this conflict?
- What did you learn about yourself and your way of dealing with conflict?

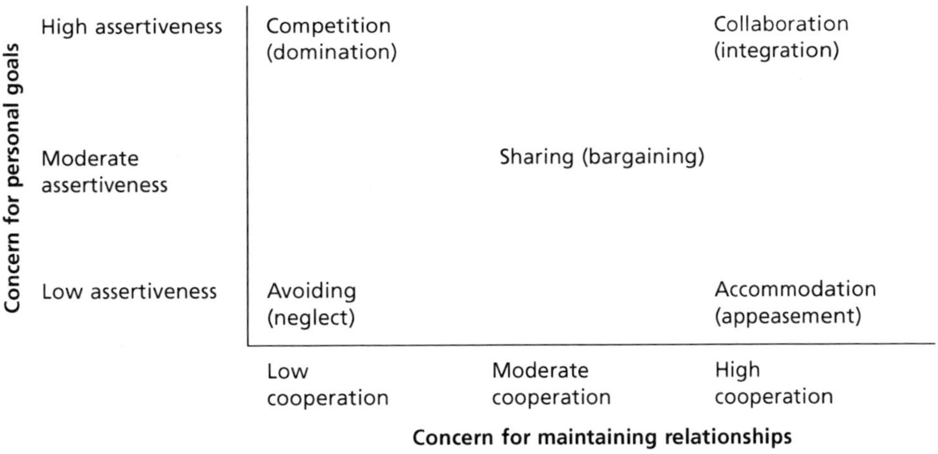

Figure 7.3 Resolution styles which may be evident during conflict management (adapted from Thomas, 1976)

Table 7.3 Conflict resolution styles

What could you do?	Positive perceptions	Negative perceptions
You could withdraw into your shell and *avoid* the situation.	• By withdrawing from the situation, you simply don't have to deal with it. • By ignoring those with whom you are in conflict, you avoid unpleasantness.	• You could be seen as weak and not sufficiently proactive.
You could try to overpower the opposition and *compete* in order to win.	• You might be seen as strong and purposeful. • Useful when having to get involved or eliciting information.	• You might be seen as intimidating and aggressive – even a bully.
You could try to build and maintain relationships in order to *accommodate* the views of others.	• You might be liked and respected for your warm feelings.	• You might be accused of papering over obvious cracks by encouraging everyone to stay friends.
You could try to seek out the middle ground and *share* the spoils.	• You might be seen as being prepared to give up part of your goals in order to achieve compromise.	• You might be seen as indecisive and weak.
You could look for a pragmatic solution and through *collaboration* satisfy the needs of all parties.	• You might be seen as someone who considers all the options before solving the conflict issue.	• You may be accused of taking too long to reach a solution.

Point for reflection

The purpose of this activity (adapted from Hall, Wallace and Hill, 1991) is to raise your awareness, in greater detail, of your conflict management style. Choose and retain a single frame of reference, e.g. work-related conflicts with team members, before answering all 15 items. Allocate 10 points among the four alternative answers given for the 15 items below. For example:

EXAMPLE

When the people I supervise become involved in a personal conflict, I usually:	
a. *intervene to settle the dispute*	3
b. *call a meeting to talk over the problem*	4
c. *offer to help if I can*	3
d. *ignore the problem*	0
1. When someone *I care about* is actively hostile toward me, i.e. yelling, threatening, abusive, etc., I tend to: a. respond in a hostile manner b. try to persuade the person to give up his/her actively hostile behaviour c. stay and listen as long as possible d. walk away	
2. When someone who is relatively *unimportant* to me is actively hostile toward me, i.e. yelling, threatening, abusive, etc., I tend to: a. respond in a hostile manner b. try to persuade the person to give up his/her actively hostile behaviour c. stay and listen as long as possible d. walk away	
3. When I observe people in conflicts in which anger, threats, hostility and strong opinions are present, I tend to: a. become involved and take a position b. attempt to mediate c. observe to see what happens d. leave as quickly as possible	
4. When I perceive another person as meeting his/her needs at my expense, I am apt to: a. work to do anything I can to change that person b. rely on persuasion and 'facts' when attempting to have the person change c. work hard at changing how I relate to that person d. accept the situation as it is	
5. When involved in an interpersonal dispute, my general pattern is to: a. draw the other person into seeing the problem as I do b. examine the issues between us as logically as possible	

c. look hard for a workable compromise

d. let time take its course and let the problem work itself out

6. The quality that I value the most in dealing with conflict would be:

a. emotional strength and security

b. intelligence

c. love and openness

d. patience

7. Following a serious altercation with someone I care for deeply, I:

a. strongly desire to go back and settle things my way

b. want to go back and work it out – whatever give-and-take is necessary

c. worry about it a lot but not plan to initiate further contact

d. let it lie and not plan to initiate further contact

8. When I see a serious conflict developing between two people I care about, I tend to:

a. express my disappointment that this had to happen

b. attempt to persuade them to resolve their differences

c. watch to see what develops

d. leave the scene

9. When I see a serious conflict developing between two people who are relatively unimportant to me, I tend to:

a. express my disappointment that this had to happen

b. attempt to persuade them to resolve their differences

c. watch to see what develops

d. leave the scene

10. The feedback that I receive from most people about how I behave when faced with conflict and opposition indicates that I:

a. try hard to get my way

b. try to work out differences cooperatively

c. am easygoing and take a soft or conciliatory position

d. usually avoid the conflict

11. When communicating with someone with whom I am having a serious conflict, I:

a. try to overpower the other person with my speech

b. talk a little bit more than I listen

c. am an active listener (feeding back words and feelings)

d. am a passive listener (agreeing and synchronizing)

12. When involved in an unpleasant conflict, I:

a. use humour with the other party

b. make an occasional quip or joke about the situation or the relationship

   c. relate humour only to myself

   d. suppress all attempts at humour

13. When someone does something that irritates me, my tendency in communicating with the offending person is to:
    a. insist that the person look me in the eye
    b. look the person directly in the eye and maintain eye contact
    c. maintain intermittent eye contact
    d. avoid looking directly at the person

14. When someone does something that irritates me, my tendency in communicating with the offending person is to:
    a. stand close and make physical contact
    b. use my hands and body to illustrate my points
    c. stand close to the person without touching him or her
    d. stand back and keep my hands to myself

15. When someone does something that irritates me, my tendency in communicating with the offending person is to:
    a. use strong direct language and tell the person to stop
    b. try to persuade the person to stop
    c. talk gently and tell the person what my feelings are
    d. say and do nothing

Scoring

When you have completed all 15 items, add up the 15 scores for the (a) answers and insert them in Column 1, the 15 scores for (b) in Column 2, and so on.

Totals:	Column 1	Column 2	Column 3	Column 4
	A =	B =	C =	D =

Using your total scores in each column, fill in the bar graph below.

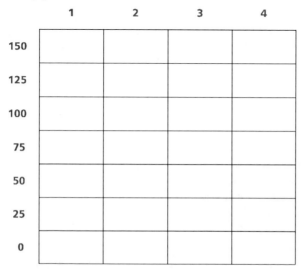

Interpretation

- Column 1: Aggressive/confrontational – High scores indicate a tendency towards 'taking the bull by the horns' and a strong need to control situations and/or people. Those who use this style are often directive and judgemental.
- Column 2: Assertive/persuasive – High scores indicate a tendency to stand up for oneself without being pushy, a proactive approach to conflict, and a willingness to collaborate. People who use this style depend heavily on their verbal skills.
- Column 3: Observant/introspective – High scores indicate a tendency to observe others and examine oneself analytically in response to conflict situations as well as a need to adopt synchronizing and listening modes of behaviour. Those who use this style are likely to be cooperative, even conciliatory.
- Column 4: Avoiding/reactive – High scores indicate a tendency toward passivity or withdrawal in conflict situations and a need to avoid confrontation. Those who use this style are usually accepting and patient, often suppressing their strong feelings.

Now total your scores for Columns 1 and 2, and Columns 3 and 4:

Column 1 + Column 2 = Score A
Column 3 + Column 4 = Score B

If Score 'A' is significantly higher than Score 'B' (25 points or more), it may indicate a tendency toward aggressive/assertive conflict management. A significantly higher 'B' score signals a more conciliatory approach.

From this activity, you will have recognized yourself as preferring one of the four conflict management styles described. Does your perception of your own style match with colleagues' perceptions of you? Which of these four broad categories do you think is most effective for resolving the kinds of conflict you encounter in your team?

The profile shows you where you are now. Does it tell you anything about where you want to go?

IS CONFLICT ALWAYS NEGATIVE? CAN CONFLICT EVER BE CONSTRUCTIVE?

Conflict is not always negative. In fact, it can be healthy, but only when effectively managed. Conflict can help the team grow and develop by:

Clearing the air!

Conflict is a valuable means for releasing highly-charged feelings. The alternative, for some, is to hold their negative emotions so much in check that they experience high levels of stress. By bringing these feelings into the open they can alleviate some of the harmful effects caused by stress. Effective team leaders, who are in sync with their team members, recognize the symptoms of escalating stress levels and offer opportunity to resolve the conflict.

Building self-confidence

Resolving conflict situations successfully, provides us with greater confidence for dealing with further situations that might arise in the future. Furthermore, the learning that takes place as a result of our involvement equips us with a rich resource of personal management skills that can be deployed as required.

Asserting principles

Sharing our thoughts and insights offers others a glimpse of the importance we attach to particular issues. It helps our team colleagues and others appreciate where we stand on things. Furthermore, it enriches the debate.

Improving status and respect

Being perceived as an assertive individual who, by demonstrating a fair and consistent style, is able to participate in debate in a lucid and balanced way will help you gain the respect of those around you.

Encouraging recognition

People who deal with conflict effectively will often gain recognition from senior managers. Mastering the skill of conflict management can be highly advantageous when being considered for more senior positions.

WHAT IF ALL ELSE FAILS AND CONFLICT CONTINUES?

Because teams fall into patterns of behaviour come what may, team leaders have a responsibility to agree strategies between themselves and members of the team. The most productive way of doing this is in a transparent and honest way during a team meeting. Agree some ground rules for dealing with conflict. Fox (2002) offers some useful guidelines for doing so, outlined in Table 7.4.

WHAT COPING STRATEGIES SHOULD I EMPLOY TO DEAL WITH A DIFFICULT TEAM MEMBER WHO REFUSES TO PERFORM?

When you are unable to understand immediately what is going on because someone is relaying confusing messages or appears to be hostile, establishing and maintaining rapport is crucial. You can do this by:

- maintaining eye contact;
- mirroring the person's body language;
- speaking at the same pace in the same tone and at the same volume;
- synchronizing your breathing; and
- using the same language.

Table 7.4 'dos' and 'don'ts for dealing with ongoing conflict

Do	Don't
Establish ground rules for dealing with conflict as soon as possible – arrange a meeting to do so.	**Hope that conflict won't occur** – adopting an ostrich mentality really doesn't work.
Bring conflict out at the earliest 'safe' time – when you feel that the team is ready to deal with conflict in an adult way. Look for the 'moment of truth', i.e. a moment when a solution is possible.	**Emphasize negative aspects of conflict** – if you tell others that you find conflict difficult, they may take advantage. Set an example and behave in an adult way.
Remain impartial – 'stay on the fence' while you are investigating the situation.'	**Avoid conflict** – it is best to bite the bullet and deal with it.
Encourage team ownership of outcomes – the more people that 'buy in' to the outcome the better.	**Allow conflict to fester** – like an untreated wound it will only get worse and take longer to heal.
Be realistic and honest – you need to live in the real world and admit that there is a difference of opinion, approach or perception. Commitment to the truth is valued.	**Personalize conflict** – don't turn into a slanging match. Keep it about work, not personalities.
Resolve the difficulty to the satisfaction of both parties – not 'I win, you lose' but 'We solved the problem together'.	**Trivialize the other person's anger or strong emotions** – the issue may not be all that important to you, but for others it may seem a matter of life or death.
Communicate – keep talking to your team. In regular one-to-one meetings you can often nip problems in the bud, encourage good performance and get to know individuals. Listen to concerns.	**Add to the emotional side of conflict situations** – individual owning solutions could mean that the team becomes fragmented. There needs to be a cohesive response that strengthens the team.
Use a systematic approach to problem solving – consistency engenders trust.	
Use assertiveness techniques to maintain your rights without violating other people's – behaving as an adult, rational being shows that you are open to the needs of others.	
Attack the problem not the person – more often than not, conflict situations arise because of how we do something. Focus on the issues not the personalities.	
Allow the other side to let off steam – clarify expectations and roles. Listen actively and acknowledge what is being said.	
Speak about yourself not about them – use 'I' statements. Own the problem and how it affects you.	
Make your proposals consistent with other people's values – synchronize with where other people are coming from. Never forget the 'WIIFM' (What's In It For Me) factor.	
Focus on interests not positions – behind opposing positions lie shared and compatible interests, as well as conflicting ones. Be hard on the problem not the person.	

As rapport grows, so will the empathy you have with your colleague. When empathy has been established, you will begin to predict how he or she will respond in future.

BUT, IF THERE SIMPLY IS NO WARNING, HOW DO I TAKE THE HEAT OUT OF A CONFLICT SITUATION?

Taking the immediate heat out of conflict situations, where people are behaving aggressively, is important because it is only when you have calmed the person down that you will be able to regain their attention and move the discussion forward productively. A particularly helpful way of achieving this is by diverting the person's attention by posing a question that requires thought. For example, the tactic will cause the person to look at the issues one step removed from both of you. Further 'cooling' time can be gained if you work through the issues together using an 'issues grid' (an example is shown in Figure 7.4). This method enables you both to gather facts and move the focus from the problem you both face to the actions that need to be taken to secure resolution of the problem.

ISSUES GRID				
Analysis	Scale of problem	Current situation	Desired situation	Action needed

Figure 7.4 **An example of an issues grid**

Point for reflection
How would you make use of an 'issues grid' to enable you and a difficult person to identify difficulties involved and work on devising a solution?

If the 'diversion' tactic is helping you to make progress, decide on the behaviour that you would now wish to cultivate in your team colleague and gradually alter aspects of your own body language to try to encourage it. When your colleague starts mirroring you, then you are establishing increasing rapport and can move the person from a negative stance to a positive one. Just in case things don't work out as well as they should, adopt the two-option rule. Always provide your colleague with an escape route. Difficult individuals do not like being cornered. Allowing them some freedom to establish their own objectives and timescales within your agreed framework is vital.

Point for reflection
For each of the following scenarios propose ways in which the situation might be best handled during and following the incident.

Case study 1

One of your team is always quiet and sullen during team meetings. You are aware that they do not like having to conduct the area audit survey. While the other team members participate in the meeting, exchanging good ideas and helping one another sort out problems, this person sits in silence.

Case study 2

You have a temporary teacher to cover a maternity leave. You need them to participate in the data collection for the area. They are openly cynical about asking the pupils for feedback, but as a new member of staff they have not been briefed for the purpose.

Case study 3

You are planning some important changes in the subject area's assessment policy. While you have made most of these decisions in the past, you know that your team has some definite ideas about assessment. Your team has been working well and harmoniously for over a year. In the past, they have resolved the few personality conflicts that have occurred.

SUMMARY SELF-REVIEW

Spend a little time considering and then responding to the following review questions:

1. How well do I know my team members and what motivates them?

2. How closely do I observe the behaviours of my team and look for signs of disagreement and conflict?

3. How well do I know the strengths and weaknesses of my team members?

4. How familiar am I with the learning styles of individual team members?

5. How successful am I at creating a climate that builds trust and confidence?

6. How sincerely do I greet the people with whom I work?

7. How effective am I in encouraging team members to give feedback both to me and to each other?

8. How successfully do I share information with my team and check their understanding of important matters?

9. How well am I encouraging the team to focus on the needs of students and the importance of teaching and learning?

10. How confident am I that individual team members know what their specific roles and responsibilities are?

11. How well do I define a problem and plan how to overcome it by generating options?

12. What is my normal approach to dealing with difficult people? How successful am I?

13. How assertive am I in conflict situations?

14. How carefully do I listen to others?

15. How do I decide when the time is right to confront difficult people and when it is wise to avoid confrontation?

16. How sensitive am I to body language that signals confrontation?

17. How do I deal with objections from my team to my suggestions?

18. Do I know when to be flexible and when to hold my ground?

Action planning

Having spent some time reviewing your approach to handling conflict, identify some actions that you might take to strengthen your current approach.

8 Leading the Team through Strategic Decision-making

Nothing is more difficult, and therefore more precious than to be able to decide.
(Napolean)

INTRODUCTION

Decisions, and the process of decision-making, are fundamental to all leadership and management processes. A significant part of any team leader's role is to make a series of decisions – some small, others much more significant. According to Warwick (1983): 'Decision-making is so much part of daily life in any school that it can easily be taken for granted. Only when things go wrong, when bad decisions have been taken or the consultation process has broken down, do most teachers become aware of it.' This chapter looks at the principles and mechanics that lie behind successful decision-making and provides useful guidance by responding to the following key questions posed by team leaders:

➤ What is decision-making?

➤ What if I lack confidence when making decisions?

➤ Are there different kinds of decisions? What are they?

➤ What are the key steps to arriving at a decision?

➤ Is there such a thing as a preferred decision-making style? How do I know what mine is?

➤ So, which is the most effective?

➤ What effect does team culture have on decision-making?

➤ How widely should I consult before arriving at a decision?

➤ Is it acceptable to delegate some decisions?

➤ Are there analytical tools I could use to help with decision-making?

➤ How can I encourage my team members to contribute creative ideas in support of the decision-making process?

➤ How can I be confident that new ideas will work? What steps can I take to try to ensure success?

➤ How do I implement decisions successfully? How do I communicate decisions to the team?

➤ How can I monitor the progress and impact of decisions?

WHAT IS DECISION-MAKING?

A decision is a judgement or choice between two or more alternatives and arises in an infinite number of situations, from the resolution of a problem to the implementation of a course of action. A decision can, of course, be made instantly but more often than not, involves team leaders in a process of identification, analysis, evaluation, choice and planning. Hall and Oldroyd (1990) suggest that 'decision-making is intimately bound up with every individual manager's personal values, personal goals and management style'. As we know, team leaders are regularly 'thinking on their feet' and making decisions throughout the school day and beyond. Most decision-making involves problem-solving and team leaders can arrive at their answers in a variety of ways. For example, there might be clear and correct answers based on facts and figures; some answers may feel right because they are based on insight borne of experience; other answers may seem satisfactory but only time will tell; and yet more will be distinctly fuzzy answers and their success may or may not emerge over time.

Point for reflection

Recall a recent significant decision that you have made and respond to the following questions:

- What did you decide?
- What helped you come to this decision?
- What hindered you?
- What did you feel about the decision you made?
- How much time did you have to make the decision?
- Who else was involved?
- Did it seem like a 'gut' decision, a rational decision, the only possible decision, a 'leap in the dark' decision?
- Do you believe you were consultative or dictatorial in reaching the decision?
- How was the decision communicated to others?
- With hindsight, would you say you made the right or wrong decision?

WHAT IF I LACK CONFIDENCE WHEN MAKING DECISIONS?

Making decisions can be a scary and uncomfortable process at times. You might be worried about the impact of your decision on others; anxious about the changes, stress, and conflict that your decision might bring about; or nervous about the results of making a 'bad' decision. Decision-making should be an exciting and motivating activity – you are making choices about what you want for your team and the students they teach. Understanding how different decision-making styles function can help you to recognize the limitations and benefits of your preferred style. There are many different ways to approach decision-making. A selection of decision-making methods is listed below:

- directive

- analytical

- conceptual

- behavioural

- impulsive

- procrastinating

- flexible

- proactive

- fatalistic

- dependent

The list could go on and on! If you have already analysed your preferred decision-making style, you will already have some understanding of how you prefer to make decisions.

Point for reflection

Read through the following paired statements and indicate with a tick those which you think best describe how you make decisions.

I like making decisions.	I don't like making decisions.
I prefer to work with colleagues when reaching a decision.	It is my job to make decisions and then to communicate them to colleagues.
When I am making a decision I often use my intuition.	When I am making a decision I tend to analyse matters closely.
I find that it helps to go back to basics and restate the issue when making a decision.	I take the basic issues as fixed when making a decision.
In my view there is little value in imagining the consequences of decisions I make.	I look to the future and try to see the consequences of decisions I make.
A good decision is one that is made quickly.	Good decisions emerge over time and must not be rushed.
Before reaching a decision, I collect as much information as possible.	I find that having more data can make reaching a decision more difficult.
I like to get ideas from other sources before making a decision.	Good decisions should not be based on other people's decisions in the same situations.

I ensure that my interests are looked after when reaching a decision.	I try to be objective and fair to others when making a decision.
It is important that I do not admit to making a mistake when a decision proves wrong.	I find that it helps to acknowledge my mistakes and to learn from them.
I take decisions in a positive manner expecting there to be a successful outcome.	I approach decisions hesitantly expecting to run into difficulties.
I take decisions differently in different circumstances.	I adopt the same approach to decisions in all circumstances.

ARE THERE DIFFERENT KINDS OF DECISIONS? WHAT ARE THEY?

The various types of decisions a team leader is likely to have to make include the following:

- **Routine** – Most decisions fall into this category because they are decisions that often recur and the proven course of action has been determined over time.

- **Emergency** – These are decisions that tend to be without precedent. You are given no time to rehearse – you make the decision on the spot as events unfold.

- **Strategic** – By far the most important, these decisions involve strategic choices and are complex since they involve decisions relating to aims and objectives which then need to be converted into realistic plans.

- **Operational** – Operational decisions require quite sensitive handling since they tend to be day-to-day ones, e.g. managing people, time and space.

Point for reflection
Read the case studies and decide the action you will take. What decisions are you faced with?

Scenario 1
A parent telephones and asks for an immediate appointment. On meeting them, they say that a member of staff has accused their child of stupidity. They complain that the teacher is very weak and has not set homework regularly. You know from other comments by staff and students that there is some truth in these complaints.
   What decisions need to be made?

Scenario 2
A teacher at the school has been involved in a fight following a political argument in a local pub during the election campaign. Nobody was injured but the press have got hold of the story.
   What decisions need to be made?

Scenario 3

A new parent governor is a very strong personality and has become used to almost daily involvement in the school. She walks in whenever she likes, goes into classes, looks at work, and has been known to chip in during lessons and attempt to deal with badly behaved pupils. She means well but the staff find it unnerving.

What decisions need to be made?

WHAT ARE THE KEY STEPS TO ARRIVING AT A DECISION?

To arrive at an effective decision is relatively simple, as long as your approach is rational and organized. Team leaders might find it helpful to follow the following five-stage plan shown in Table 8.1 to help them organize their thoughts.

Table 8.1 The five stages to successful decision-making

Stage	What does it involve?
Stage 1 – define the purpose of the action	Having recognized the need for a decision, specify the aim or objective, i.e. what exactly has to be decided?
Stage 2 – collect the information	Collect and organize data, check facts and opinions, identify possible causes, and establish time constraints and other criteria, i.e. what information do I need to help me?
Stage 3 – list the options available	List possible courses of action and generate ideas, i.e. what are the alternatives that I have to choose from?
Stage 4 – choose between the options	List the pros and cons, examine the consequences, measure against criteria, trial and test against the original objective, and select the best, i.e. what alternative is the best?
Stage 5 – convert the choice into action	Take action to carry out the decision, monitor the decision and review its impact, i.e. what action needs to be taken?

IS THERE SUCH A THING AS A PREFERRED DECISION-MAKING STYLE? HOW DO I KNOW WHAT MINE IS?

Each of us has an individual style for arriving at decisions. Some people are quite logical in their approach to decision-making; others are creative. Research shows (e.g. Covey, 1989) that one side of our brain is the location of emotion, imagination, intuition and creativity, while the other is the site of logic, language, and analysis. Though people tend to have a dominant side, this does not mean that decision-makers fall into two distinct categories. Whichever side our natural decision-making style leans towards, we need to try to achieve a balance between both sets of faculties. Therefore, the way in which decisions are made can be grouped into two different categories: rational and intuitive (Table 8.2).

Table 8.2 The characteristics of rational and intuitive thinkers

Rational thinkers have the following characteristics	Intuitive thinkers have the following characteristics
• they follow a logical process • the problem that needs a decision is identified and defined • all the alternatives are ascertained by gathering relevant information • these alternatives are evaluated before the decision is made	• they rely on feelings to help them to make a decision • they may make impulsive decisions that 'feel right' • they may use a coin toss or a roll of a dice to determine a particular course of action • they only think about the consequences of the decision after it has been made
You will be using a rational approach if you	**You will be using an intuitive approach if you**
• draw up a list of the pros and cons • weigh up all of the options • seek more information on the alternatives • use the experience and expertise of others to help you reach your decision • use knowledge, skills and experience • apply logic to reach conclusions • analyse issues to understand the whole picture	• lead by emotion and sensitivity • use imagination to create new ideas • come to conclusions by hunch

The rational approach is called so because it relies on a logical process in order to make the decision. A person using this style will approach the decision using an objective and analytical methodology. Feelings and emotions about the decision will be put to one side while all the information is being gathered and analysed. Previous decisions may affect the intuitive decision-maker, as their decisions may be made out of habit. Some intuitive decision-makers might be quite fatalistic about decisions – 'whatever will be, will be' is an apt motto for a fatalistic decision-maker.

Point for reflection

From what you have read in this section, how would you describe your own decision-making style? Think of behaviours and attitudes that exemplify your style and approach. Try to do the same for the members of your team.

SO, WHICH IS THE MOST EFFECTIVE?

Most people will use a combination of rational and intuitive decision-making styles. You can gather all the information in the world to help you make a decision, but if it doesn't feel right, the chances are that it's not. The most important thing to remember is that you should use the approach that is most comfortable and applicable to you. However, the approach still needs to be appropriate to the decision being made. You would not necessarily write up a list of pros and cons to help you decide what to have for your dinner, and neither would you toss a coin to help you decide whether to apply for a deputy headship! Don't be afraid of combining the two approaches and using as many different styles as you need to. Whatever your preferred style, good decisions tend to have the following characteristics:

- they offer realistic expectations;
- they allow for flexibility and modification;
- they are consistent with your goals and values; and
- they relate directly to the problem.

'Bad' decisions are often made when you:

- don't analyse all the necessary information;
- feel rushed into making a decision;
- make a decision for somebody else;
- don't have control over the process; and
- are not clear about why you need to make that decision.

WHAT EFFECT DOES TEAM CULTURE HAVE ON DECISION-MAKING?

The school's, and ultimately, the team's culture is a strong influence on the decision-making process because it affects so many of the issues and options. Team leaders will need to be aware of what is and what is not acceptable. For example, in a school where the culture is 'authoritarian' there may be an over-reliance on bureaucracy and therefore your latitude for making 'exciting' decisions may well be restricted. In innovative schools, you may be expected to be more adventurous – even risky – in terms of the decisions you take.

Point for reflection
To assess the nature of the culture that dominates your school/team, consider the statements in Table 8.3 and see which of them best fit your situation.

HOW WIDELY SHOULD I CONSULT BEFORE ARRIVING AT A DECISION?

Whom to consult, and how, is, of course, one of your first decisions. Look for specific expertise and experience related to the issues upon which a decision needs to be made. Having weighed the advice, check that you have full autonomy to proceed. If not, consult with line managers – not just for their approval but also their input. Even if you do not need to have your decision sanctioned, bear in mind that they are much more likely to lend their support if they have been kept in the picture. Always try to recognize the contribution

Table 8.3 Characteristics of risk avoiders and risk takers

Risk avoiders	Risk takers
• New ideas are often dismissed.	• New and creative ideas are welcomed.
• The school/team is not always driven by external needs.	• The school/team focuses mainly on the needs of students.
• The emphasis within the school/team is on dealing with problems.	• The school/team's main emphasis is on taking advantage of new opportunities.
• Suitability and experience are the most valued attributes of the school/team.	• Motivation and innovation are highly valued characteristics.
• The success of the school/team is put before the success of students.	• School/team and individual needs are largely aligned.
• Command and control appear to be the dominant processes.	• All staff are allowed autonomy and encouraged to display initiative.
• It is very difficult to change the school/team mindset.	• Minds and policies are often changed according to circumstances.
If you agree with most of the above, your school/team is definitely averse to taking risks. Decisions involving new ideas are not welcomed readily.	If you agree with the most of the above, your school/team is forward-looking, not afraid of change and content to take bold decisions that create success.

made by team members, however small. Consultation with team members is particularly helpful because it can improve the effectiveness with which decisions are reached in at least two ways:

• those whom you approach for their views should be able to make a useful contribution to the process; and

• the chances of implementing your decision successfully are heightened if people know what they are doing and have been influential in the process.

There are, of course, a few pitfalls associated with consulting others. First, there is the issue of time. The more you consult, the longer the decision-making process will take. In addition, bear in mind that the more people you consult with, the higher your chances of being confused by the mass of views – some no doubt contradictory – you will receive. Secondly, if too many people become involved you may well lose your grip over the whole process. Maintain your control over the process by consulting with only a small number of the 'right' people – those who are prepared to be honest and who have a representative spread of views. Display positive listening throughout. This means more than just hearing what is being said. Understand the significance of what is being said because this will enable you to make decisions based on a real understanding of the attitudes of others. Table 8.4 shows the three levels of involvement, the styles most likely to be utilized at each level and the conditions under which they are most likely to be used.

Table 8.4 Consulting with others: the three levels of involvement

Methods	Characteristics	When used
Low involvement These decisions are taken by leaders with seniority and are low on consultation.	*Telling*: team leader takes unilateral decision without consultation	• Deadlines are tight • In emergency situations
	Selling: team leader takes decision, but others may question appropriateness	• Hard-sell is needed • Consensus unlikely
	Presenting: staff are allowed to hear the progress of discussions	• Team leader has strong views • Colleagues need to be informed
Medium involvement Final decision is taken by team leaders, but team members are consulted.	*Suggesting*: team leader puts forward choices for discussion and may be flexible over own opinion	• Views of team members are needed to help discussion and decision
	Consulting: team members' views are sought before any input from team leader, but team leader has final say	• Decision needs specialist input
High involvement The decision-making process is democratic, with all team members invited to participate.	*Asking*: team leader establishes parameters to be discussed, but responsibility for the decision rests with the team	• Best decision requires the input and full involvement of team
	Participating: team members come together to discuss options and make decision by consensus	• Commitment to the final decision is crucial to the success of the plan

IS IT ACCEPTABLE TO DELEGATE SOME DECISIONS?

Delegating decisions offers team members excellent professional development opportunities. The most important consideration for team leaders is to decide which decisions to make yourself and which to delegate to others. Effective decision-makers distribute and share responsibility widely. Assess what decisions your team members are capable of taking. If the answer is none, either your assessment of the situation or your training may be at fault. A great deal will depend on your individual delegating style, but it is important to remember that you remain responsible for the decision you delegate, so oversee the delegation, especially in sensitive areas. That overview can be very useful for coaching and mentoring. Try to:

• build up the confidence of team members to whom you delegate;

• maintain a two-way flow of information;

• encourage team members to develop their own initiative; and

- not reject a decision until you have had full discussions with those concerned.

ARE THERE ANALYTICAL TOOLS I COULD USE TO HELP WITH DECISION-MAKING?

To reach a sound strategic decision it is sensible to analyse all the relevant facts. Useful analytical techniques exist to help you consider decisions from many different angles. Three of these techniques are set out here:

SWOT analysis

A SWOT analysis helps establish where your team stands within the school as a whole. Your team's Strengths, Weaknesses, Opportunities and Threats hold the key to strategic decision-making. Carrying out an analysis using the SWOT framework (Table 8.5) helps you to focus your activities on areas where you are strong and where the greatest opportunities lie. It is important to appraise the issues honestly, rather than being too modest or over-critical.

In itself, a SWOT analysis doesn't identify what should be done: rather it provides a framework for identifying where strategic opportunities may exist and how to avoid weaknesses inherent within the team/school or threats from outside limiting future growth and improvement. It also offers a useful framework to revisit when strategic decisions are being taken: how will deciding such and such impact upon the SWOT; in taking advantage of strengths and opportunities will it create additional weaknesses; or in fixing one weakness will it create an additional threat, or impact upon other strengths?

Table 8.5 SWOT analysis

STRENGTHS	WEAKNESSES
Consider these from your own point of view and from the point of view of the people you interact with. Don't be modest but be realistic.	Consider these from an internal and external basis.
What is the team competent at? *What is it really good at?* *What does it do exceptionally well?* *What are the team's advantages?*	*What could you improve?* *What do you do badly?* *Is the team short of key resources or capabilities?*
OPPORTUNITIES	**THREATS**
Look at your strengths and ask yourself whether these open any opportunities. Look at your weaknesses and ask whether you could open up opportunities by eliminating them.	Identify those factors, both internal and external, local and national, that might threaten the strategic direction and viability of what you are attempting to do.
Can the team improve its present performance? *What could we do?*	*What threatens the present performance of the team?* *How real are these threats?* *How immediate are they?*

Cause-and-effect diagram or fishbone diagram

This technique is also known as 'fishboning' (Figure 8.1) or as an Ishikawa diagram after its inventor Kaoru Ishikawa, who first used the technique in the 1960s. The diagram is a structured and analytical method of identifying, categorizing and prioritizing all the causes of a given situation. These causes are then targeted for improvement. The technique can be used to explain an existing situation or to identify the factors necessary to create a desired new situation.

The basic concept in the cause-and-effect diagram is that the name of a basic problem, issue or area of interest is entered at the right of the diagram at the end of the main 'bone'. The main possible causes of the problem (the effect) are drawn as bones arising from the main backbone. It is important to identify causes rather than symptoms at this point. Different names can be chosen to suit the problem at hand, or the general categories (e.g. assignments) can be revised. The key is to have three to six main categories that encompass all possible influences. Brainstorming is typically done to add possible causes to the main bones and more specific causes to the smaller bones. This subdivision into ever-increasing specificity continues as long as the problem areas can be further subdivided. The practical maximum depth of this fishbone is usually about four or five levels. When the fishbone is complete, it offers a detailed picture of all the possibilities that could be the root cause for the designated problem. The cause-and-effect diagram can be used by individuals, but probably most effectively by a team. Once the entire fishbone is complete, team discussion takes place to decide what are the most likely root causes of the problem. These causes are usually circled to indicate items that should be acted upon.

Force field analysis

Force field analysis is a useful technique developed by Kurt Lewin (1951), a pioneer in the field of social sciences, for analysing perceptions of the forces working for or against a particular task, process or decision. It can be completed individually or by a group. The technique requires the identification of those forces that help the achievement of a particular outcome and those forces that hinder. By carrying out the analysis you can plan to strengthen the forces supporting a decision, and reduce the impact of opposition to it. To carry out a force field analysis, you need to follow these steps:

- List all forces that are helping change in one column, and all forces hindering change in the other (Figure 8.2).
- Assign a score to each force, from 1 (weak) to 5 (strong).
- Draw a diagram showing the forces for and against change. Show the size of each force as a number next to it.
- Once you have carried out an analysis, you can decide whether your project is viable.

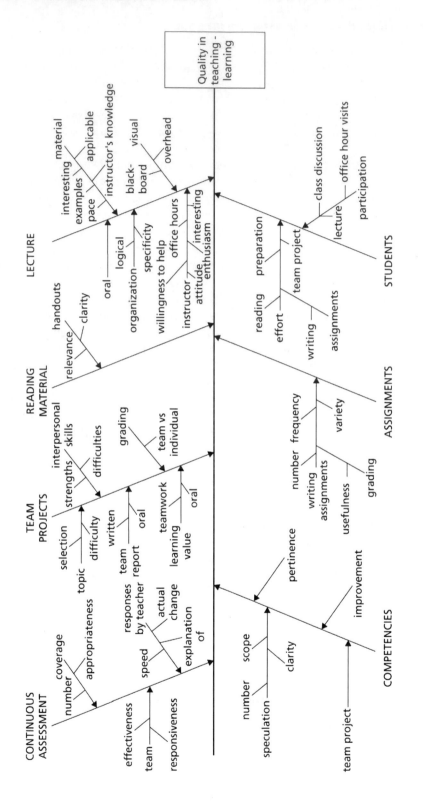

Figure 8.1 Cause-and-effect diagram of quality in teaching and learning (*Source:* University of Wolverhampton, School of Education, Research Methods Module – Study Materials.)

SCORE	HELPING	HINDERING	SCORE

Figure 8.2 Force field analysis

Where you have already decided to carry out a project, force field analysis can help you to work out how to improve its probability of success. Here you have two choices: to reduce the strength of the forces hindering or opposing a project, or to increase the forces helping or pushing a project.

Point for reflection

Apply one or all of the above techniques to a problem or issue you and your team currently face.

HOW CAN I ENCOURAGE MY TEAM MEMBERS TO CONTRIBUTE CREATIVE IDEAS IN SUPPORT OF THE DECISION-MAKING PROCESS?

For any team, but particularly well-established ones, the creation of new ideas is vital to bring a fresh view to the decision-making process. As a team leader, you are looking for ideas that have a blend of imagination and practicality. Do you have anyone in your team that is capable of thinking 'outside the box'? Team meetings and training days offer excellent opportunities for generating ideas. Choose a topic and define the issues that require decisions. Invite each team member to submit an idea relevant to that area. Record each idea – even outlandish ones – and do not reject any. Value them all at this stage. The more ideas generated the better, but do not judge or analyse them at this point. Now revisit each idea and select ideas that are worthy of further investigation and follow-up. You will probably recognize the above process as 'brainstorming'. To get the best results from this technique consider doing the following:

- prepare your team members by identifying the topic or issue under consideration and ask them to come to the meeting prepared to present two or three ideas each;

- offer each team member, in turn, the chance to air their views on the topic or issue;

- don't impose too many constraints on the way in which your colleagues share creative ideas;

- limit interruptions and stick to the subject in question;

- provide the team with a few ideas of your own – this will help direct discussions and act as a stimulus for others;

- try to encourage logical thought and lateral thinking to break down long-held preconceptions;

- cluster all the ideas generated so that you end up with groups of linked ideas;

- start to create a shortlist of the best ideas; and

- above all, never criticize any of the ideas in front of your team.

HOW CAN I BE CONFIDENT THAT NEW IDEAS WILL WORK? WHAT STEPS CAN I TAKE TO TRY TO ENSURE SUCCESS?

After generating some ideas, you will need to gauge their potential for achieving what you want them to achieve. To enable you to do so, you will need objective criteria and a rational approach. The *'what if?'* analysis may be of some help here when it comes to assessing the value of ideas. To carry out a 'what if?' analysis, think of an idea and ask yourself what would be the likely consequences of adopting it. Try to approach it from different angles, so that you cover most eventualities.

Point for reflection
Your team has proposed that, instead of the present hierarchical model of lesson observation, the subject area should institute a 'peer observation' model. Use the 'what if?' analysis to assess the value of this idea. The analysis should help you answer the question: What would a change from 'top-down' to 'peer' observation actually mean?

The majority of decisions contain a certain level of uncertainty and risk. Your experience and professional judgement will go some considerable way towards removing some doubt but there is still a need to assess consequences.

HOW DO I IMPLEMENT DECISIONS SUCCESSFULLY? HOW DO I COMMUNICATE DECISIONS TO THE TEAM?

Decisions, however skilfully arrived at, are of little value unless they are converted into positive action, usually by means of a plan of action. A plan of action will begin to evolve naturally as options are discussed and narrowed by the team. Involving others, and using their relevant skills, in developing a plan is crucial. Effective plans benefit from detailed actions; clear starting and completion dates; realistic milestones for key events; specific outcomes; and break points at which action can be reviewed and revised. A possible format for such a plan is shown in Figure 8.3.

TEAM ACTION PLAN

Area/Team:				Team Leader:			Date:
Start date	Objectives/ targets	Action needed	Staff	Resources/ INSET	Success criteria	Completion date

Figure 8.3 **Example of a team action plan**

Sharing information with everyone involved in the implementation of the decision is part of the team leader's responsibility. Team members need to understand exactly what has been decided and why, and their support ecouraged. When you make your decision, provide explanations about the alternative courses of action you have considered and the reasons why, in the end, you went for the option you did. Make it clear how the decision will impact on team members but also on the school and the students in their care. Try not to be defensive if questioned about the decision and also try to make changes in response to genuine concerns or better ideas. Always welcome contribution from anybody who will be affected by your decision. Having communicated the decision, it is important to keep the team abreast of progress throughout the implementation of the decision. Team meetings, informal or formal, are good opportunities to do this (Figure 8.4).

HOW CAN I MONITOR THE PROGRESS AND IMPACT OF DECISIONS?

Once a decision has been taken and put into action, even the most thorough of plans encounter some, often unforeseen, difficulties. Monitoring progress to ensure that difficulties are spotted and effective remedies put in place becomes a crucial role for team leaders. You need to check the progress of the project regularly, either at natural milestones, or at other specific intervals to ensure that the decision taken is still the right one. A well-constructed action plan, an

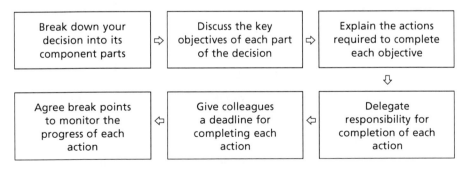

Figure 8.4 **Clarifying decisions for team members**

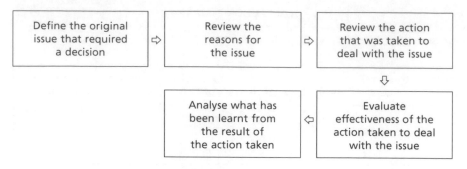

Figure 8.5 **Monitoring progress and impact**

outline of which is shown in Figure 8.5, is invaluable for tracking progress. The plan also offers you a basis for assessing the effectiveness of the decision taken, using the process shown.

SUMMARY SELF-REVIEW

Spend a little time considering and then responding to the following review questions:

1. How effective am I in making decisions and ensuring that they are implemented?

2. How carefully and fully do I analyse situations before taking decisions?

3. How readily do I delegate decisions that do not have to be taken by me?

4. How effectively do I combine intellectual and creative approaches to decision-making?

5. How aware am I of the kind of decision that I am taking before starting the process?

6. How successfully do I make use of my understanding of team culture to get support for my decisions?

7. How well do I prioritize significant factors that relate to the decision area?

8. How do I create the widest possible involvement for my team in the decision-making process?

9. How appropriately do I consult prior to making a decision?

10. How well do I prepare my ideas before making a case to the team?

11. How effectively do I judge alternatives against the criteria that the decision must satisfy?

12. How systematically do I gather available information to inform decision-making?

13. How fully do I consider the actions and reactions that affect and follow from my decisions?

14. How well do I weigh up probabilities when considering forecasts and planned outcomes?

15. How readily do I take necessary risks when arriving at a decision?

16. Do I take decisions on their merits?

17. How regularly do I involve the team in drawing up plans for implementation?

18. How openly, honestly and swiftly do I communicate my decisions?

19. How effective are my monitoring procedures?

Action planning

Having spent some time reviewing your approach to making strategic decisions, identify some actions that you might take to strengthen your current approach.

9 Conducting Effective Performance Management Reviews

The performance management review . . . is concerned above all with improving the skills of teachers so that they in turn can raise the levels of performance of the pupils they teach . . .

(Dean, 2002)

INTRODUCTION

Within schools, and in a range of other organizations, significant developments have taken place in an effort to dispense with the one-off annual appraisal and replace it with a more dynamic, ongoing process of performance management through objective setting and continuing professional development. Whereas some organizations have introduced performance ratings and performance-related pay schemes, others are exploring the use of competences, peer appraisal and 360 degree feedback as methods for promoting staff development. By addressing the following questions, this chapter provides comprehensive guidance on conducting effective performance management reviews:

➢ What are performance management reviews?

➢ Why conduct regular performance management reviews? What are the benefits?

➢ Why has there developed a much closer link between performance and development?

➢ What is my role as team leader in performance management reviews? What is the expectation of team members?

➢ What key factors have been found to determine the success of performance management reviews?

➢ How can I best prepare for a performance management review?

➢ Is there an easy to follow structure that I could use when conducting a review meeting?

➢ How can I help team members agree meaningful objectives?

➢ What skills do I need at a review meeting?

➢ How do I handle pauses and silences?

➤ How important is body language/non-verbal communication?

➤ How do I make notes at the review discussion and still show that I am really listening?

➤ IIow do I give feedback in a helpful and constructive way?

➤ How do I give constructive feedback in negative situations?

➤ What else should I take account of when communicating with colleagues at the review?

➤ How do I maintain a good relationship with a team member to whom I have had to give negative feedback?

WHAT ARE PERFORMANCE MANAGEMENT REVIEWS?

Performance reviews form the basis for assessing the three key elements of performance: contribution, capability and continuous development. The main intention behind the introduction of performance management in England, for example, is for schools to demonstrate a commitment to: 'develop all teachers effectively to ensure job satisfaction, high levels of expertise and progression of staff in their chosen profession' (*Performance Management in Schools*, DfEE, April 2000).

Under these mandatory arrangements, the performance review stage is the final one in the framework's three-stage performance management cycle. Performance review is preceded by two other stages – planning and monitoring (see Figure 9.1).

WHY CONDUCT REGULAR PERFORMANCE MANAGEMENT REVIEWS? WHAT ARE THE BENEFITS?

Conducting regular performance management reviews is extremely important, as it helps to build up a picture, not only of the performance of the school, but also, more particularly, of individual staff. It is crucial to carry out reviews annually, not necessarily as a result of the DfES's stipulation, but because it provides a regular scheduled opportunity for team leaders and team members to take part in genuine dialogue about:

- the reviewee's job description;

- the teacher's work, including successes and areas of development identified since the planning and agreeing of objectives earlier in the cycle;

- continuing professional development needs;

- career development, if applicable;

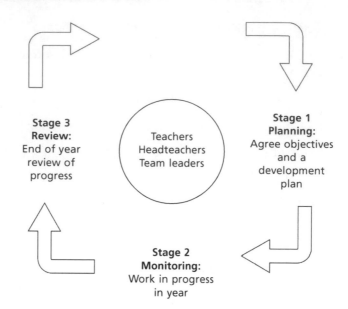

Figure 9.1   **The performance management cycle (adapted from DfEE, 2000)**

- the teacher's overall contribution to the policies and management of the school, and any constraints which the circumstances of the school place on him or her;

- objectives for future action and development; and

- points that may need to be included in the written review statement.

Point for reflection

What benefits would you wish to gain as a result of conducting performance reviews (a) for each member of your team, (b) for yourself as their team leader?

WHY HAS THERE DEVELOPED A MUCH CLOSER LINK BETWEEN PERFORMANCE AND DEVELOPMENT?

The evidence from a great deal of the research into improving school effectiveness points to the fact that teachers need support, encouragement and recognition of their achievements if they are to become more effective. Good performance management sets out to achieve this. The link between perform-ance and development has developed in recognition of the fact that you cannot alter what has happened in the past but you can significantly alter what is likely to happen in the future. By recognizing the achievements of staff, providing helpful feedback on their performance and by helping them identify areas for further development, team leaders can play a significant part in raising their self-esteem and in enhancing their skills.

WHAT IS MY ROLE AS TEAM LEADER IN PERFORMANCE MANAGEMENT REVIEWS? WHAT IS THE EXPECTATION OF TEAM MEMBERS?

The DfES's mandatory performance management arrangements (DfES, 2001b) set out a crucial team leadership role. The fundamental task for team leaders is to help others improve their performance. In summary, team leaders are expected to:

- help teachers to identify their objectives and create a development plan for achieving those objectives;

- support teachers and ensure alignment of personal objectives with department/area and school priorities;

- provide guidance, coaching and support to help staff improve their performance;

- provide regular and constructive feedback; and

- make an informed assessment about performance.

In statutory terms, team leaders and teachers are required to meet the obligations outlined in Table 9.1.

Point for reflection
From your consideration of the role of team leaders outlined above, what are the implications for your existing skill levels? In which aspects are you particularly confident? Would your team members agree? What are the areas for further skill development?

WHAT KEY FACTORS HAVE BEEN FOUND TO DETERMINE THE SUCCESS OF PERFORMANCE MANAGEMENT REVIEWS?

Review meetings are more likely to be successful when a number of key factors are present and others are eliminated, or their influence significantly reduced. In general, the following factors are pivotal:

- the skills and commitment of the team leader;

- the extent to which staff are empowered to manage their own performance;

- the quality of the relationship established between the team leader and the teacher;

Table 9.1   Statutory obligations of team leaders and teachers

Staff member	Statutory requirements
Team leaders	Team leaders must: • meet with each of the teachers for whom they are the reviewer before or at the start of the performance review cycle to plan and prepare for performance review and discuss setting objectives; • record objectives in writing and allow the job holder to add written comments if they wish; • monitor performance against these objectives throughout the year and observe the teacher teaching in the classroom at least once during the review cycle; • consult the reviewee before obtaining oral or written information from others relating to the teacher's performance; • meet with the teacher at the end of the review cycle to review performance and identify achievements, including assessment of achievement against objectives and to discuss and identify professional development needs/activities; • write a performance review statement and give a copy to the reviewee within 10 working days of the final review meeting and allow a further 10 working days for the job holder to add written comments; • pass the completed review statement to the headteacher.
Teachers	Teachers: • must meet with their team leader before or at the start of the performance review cycle to discuss setting objectives; • either agree objectives with the team leader or add written comments to the objectives recorded by the team leader; • must meet with their team leader at the end of the review cycle to review performance and identify achievement, including assessment of achievement against objectives and to discuss and identify professional development needs/activities; • may add comments to the review statement or complain about their review statement within 10 working days of receipt from the team leader.

Source: DfEE, 2000

- the extent to which staff are enabled to solve their own problems, with support from the team leader; and

- the constant focus on raising the self-esteem and capability of the teacher.

Table 9.2 identifies additional factors that help or hinder the success of review meetings.

HOW CAN I BEST PREPARE FOR A PERFORMANCE MANAGEMENT REVIEW?

Good preparation for performance review is an investment in the future performance of your team members. If the review is really to succeed, both you and the reviewee need to put considerable effort into preparing for the review. The guidelines in Table 9.3 proposed by Jones (2001) may be of some help in approaching the task.

Table 9.2 Factors affecting the success of review meetings

Factors likely to promote successful review meetings	Factors likely to militate against successful review meetings
• adequate preparation by both parties • a clearly agreed agenda • sharing of relevant data and documentation • adequate time • a limit on the number of reviews undertaken by a team leader • prompt write-up of the review statement • effective interpersonal skills • positive nature of previous relationships between the team leader and the teacher • all parties giving the review high priority • no interruptions	• inadequate time • low priority given to the review • sudden changes in planned programme • a lack of preparation by either or both parties • not keeping to the agenda • interruptions • poor prior relationships

Table 9.3 Preparation for the review meeting

The reviewer should come to the meeting:	The reviewee should come to the meeting:
• having discussed the time and venue for the meeting with the teacher • having considered the teacher's job description • with a copy of the school's agreed policy • having considered possible areas for discussion – an agenda • having prepared a strategy for structuring the discussion according to the agreed agenda • prepared to listen actively to the teacher's views and suggestions • prepared to help the reviewee to clarify the nature and meaning of the review focus • having thought of possible professional development needs and activities • with the aim of encouraging the teacher to talk constructively about key areas and of ensuring that the discussions are positive • with the aim of keeping the discussion focused on the agreed scope of the review	• having prepared by reflecting on the agreed scope of the review, the job description, the lesson observation, other supporting information and the agreed agenda • having reflected on a possible focus for the review meeting (a self-review exercise is useful preparation) • willing to discuss performance frankly and honestly • having thought of professional development needs and activities

Source: Jones, 2001

IS THERE AN EASY TO FOLLOW STRUCTURE THAT I COULD USE WHEN CONDUCTING A REVIEW MEETING?

Among the points to bear in mind when conducting the review meeting are those shown in Table 9.4. The table offers a logical sequence for team leaders to follow.

Table 9.4 Running a performance review meeting

What to do	How to do it
Prepare well	<ul><li>Conduct the review in a relaxed environment.</li><li>Avoid interruptions.</li><li>Don't hurry the proceedings.</li><li>Think through the structure of the review and consider how you will introduce each stage.</li><li>Encourage the reviewee to do most of the talking, wherever possible.</li><li>Build rapport, ask questions, listen actively and provide constructive feedback.</li></ul>
Offer a warm greeting of welcome	<ul><li>It is important to start the review meeting in a pleasant way in order to get the reviewee to relax and to establish a climate of trust and openness.</li></ul>
Explain the purpose of the review	<ul><li>Explain to the reviewee that the review meeting is intended to be supportive and developmental.</li><li>Stress that it is an opportunity for gauging success in meeting agreed objectives, discussing professional development needs, career plans, and for reviewing the job description.</li></ul>
Review the job description	<ul><li>Discuss the main tasks and responsibilities of the reviewee's role.</li><li>Decide whether the job description needs revision.</li><li>Discuss aspects of the role that have provided the greatest satisfaction and any constraints encountered.</li></ul>
Identify the positive aspects of the reviewee's work	<ul><li>Show your colleague that her/his work is valued and appreciated.</li><li>Refer specifically to areas of success rather than offering vague and general praise.</li><li>Discuss the progress made in reaching last year's agreed objectives.</li></ul>
Identify problems or areas for development	<ul><li>Invite the reviewee to identify areas of work that present problems, challenges or frustrations.</li><li>Raise problem areas that *you* have encountered, giving evidence.</li><li>Discuss ways of overcoming the problems identified.</li></ul>
Consider professional development needs and career aspirations	<ul><li>Discuss the reviewee's professional development needs (this may flow quite naturally from the previous discussion) and ways of meeting them.</li><li>Try to be imaginative about ways of meeting development needs – don't rely purely on course attendance.</li><li>Take account of any views he or she may have regarding career aspirations.</li></ul>
Agree objectives for the coming year	<ul><li>Invite suggestions from the reviewee about next year's objectives.</li><li>Suggest your own.</li><li>Ensure that they are related to team and school priorities.</li><li>Ensure that the objectives concern the progress made by pupils and the improvement of the reviewee's professional practice.</li></ul>
Agree the main content of the review statement	<ul><li>Discuss what will be included in the review statement and the date by which it will be produced.</li><li>The body of the statement should include the agreed objectives, areas of strengths and those requiring development, support and training needed.</li></ul>
Close the meeting	<ul><li>End the review by checking that both you and the reviewee feel that the ground has been covered satisfactorily.</li><li>Sum up what has been covered and agreed.</li><li>Clearly state what you are prepared to do to support the reviewee over the period of the cycle.</li><li>Re-emphasize the positive aspects of the review.</li></ul>

HOW CAN I HELP TEAM MEMBERS AGREE MEANINGFUL OBJECTIVES?

Setting and agreeing objectives is the traditional purpose of performance reviews. The objectives you agree with your team members will be more meaningful if they are:

- directly related to the team's priorities;

- specific and concise;

- stated in terms of tangible outcomes or measures;

- within the teacher's personal control;

- achievable within the resource levels;

- appropriately challenging; and

- time-framed.

The following illustrations should serve as a useful reminder of the characteristics of effective performance objectives:

S	Specific
M	Measurable
A	Achievable
R	Realistic
T	Time-framed

C	Clear
C	Concise
M	Measurable
C	Challenging
F	Flexible

The reviewee's performance is assessed against previously agreed objectives and new ones, ideally by mutual consent, are then agreed for the coming year. As a minimum, setting and agreeing objectives should take into account:

- performance against previous objectives;

- aptitude for the job;

- personal circumstances;

- future potential; and

- the changing work context.

There is little point in setting objectives that aren't measurable in terms of actual performance.

Point for reflection

In relation to the following objectives, respond to the following questions:

- To what extent is each objective:
  - clear?
  - concise?
  - measurable?
  - achievable?
  - challenging?
- If they are, how would you know?
- If not, how could they be improved?

Objective 1 *To improve the standards of writing in Year 1*
Objective 2 *To further develop ICT skills to support the effective use of data in tracking the progress of more able children*
Objective 3 *To develop strategies for improving the attainment of Year 10 de-motivated middle ability groups in geography*
Objective 4 *To improve my maths lesson plans to include appropriate challenges for high achievers in Year 6*

WHAT SKILLS DO I NEED AT A REVIEW MEETING?

Team leaders need to have a good command of a variety of interpersonal skills when conducting performance review meetings. As shown in Figure 9.2, there are four key skills involved:

- building rapport;
- questioning skills;
- listening skills; and
- feedback skills.

Building rapport

Rapport is a process of building and sustaining a relationship based on mutual trust, harmony and understanding. This happens through matching the cues

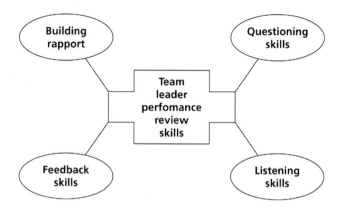

Figure 9.2 Team leader performance review skills

Table 9.5 The four levels of rapport

Level 1	Level 2	Level 3	Level 4
Non-verbal level, where you match body language, such as posture, gestures, facial expression, eye contact, etc.	*Voice level, where you match breathing rate, tone, pitch, tempo, etc.*	*Language level, where you can match process words.*	*At the level of beliefs and criteria.*

arising from the words used, eye movements and body language. Rapport is the ability to be on the same wavelength and to connect mentally and emotionally. Having rapport does not mean that you have to agree, but that you understand where the other person is coming from. It starts with acceptance of the other person's point of view, their state and their style of communication. To influence, you have to be able to appreciate and understand the other person's standpoint. And this works both ways: I cannot influence you without being open to influence myself. Having rapport as a foundation for the relationship means that when there are issues to discuss, you already have a culture in place that makes it easier to talk them through and thus to prevent issues from developing into complaints, objections or problems. There are four levels of rapport as shown in Table 9.5.

Point for reflection

How successful are you in establishing rapport with individual members of your team? Using the four levels of rapport model above, consider the levels you normally reach with individual members of your team. What might you do to establish a higher level of rapport with your team members?

Questioning skills

Good questioning technique is invaluable for team leaders when carrying out performance management reviews, for example, when attempting to unlock information, control or close conversations. When using questions it is important to be clear about the purpose you have in mind. For example, decide whether it is to:

- draw out information, knowledge, experience, opinions;
- explore feelings, attitudes;
- observe style and methods of response in order to make an assessment;
- stimulate thought;
- help the other person to think through an issue;
- clarify an issue;
- keep the discussion relevant;

- follow up a line of thought or a suggestion; and

- help the person feel more at ease.

The review meeting is very much a two-way process. There are many types of questions that can be used – some extremely useful and others that are less so, even counter-productive. However, it all depends upon which ones you use and when you use them. Basically it is about finding the right questions, which in some contexts might be:

Open questions

These are questions that invite the reviewee to talk and explore. They invite people to express their thinking clearly rather than allowing a 'yes' or 'no' or an over-simple response. Open questions help the other person to identify the issues, explore the issues and provide the team leader with information about the issues and the feelings behind them. Open questions normally begin with 'what', 'where', 'when', 'why', 'which', 'who', 'how' and 'tell me about'. Examples would be: *'What areas of development have you identified as priorities?'*, *'How do you think the training has changed your approach?'*

Closed questions

These questions elicit 'yes' or 'no' answers and are particularly useful for controlling the length and form of the reply. They can be used when confirmation of facts is required; to bring a discussion back on track; to obtain specific items of information; to test ideas that have arisen out of a period of questioning, e.g. 'Did you like . . .?', 'Have you told him . . .?' You may find it helpful to use closed questions to focus the discussion with someone who talks in general terms and who will not be precise. Wherever possible, closed questions should be interspersed with more open questions, for example: *'Did you find being on the working group interesting?'*, *'What particularly took your interest?'*

   It might be worth remembering that having used 'open' questions to elicit information, you may need to follow up by using 'closed' questions to:

- define a precise piece of information;

- firm up the opinion held by the other person; and

- achieve commitment.

Specific questions

These can be open or closed. They specify the information required through the use of nouns or numbers, e.g. *'How many children would we expect to get level 3 in maths, do you think?'*

Reflective questions

Reflecting is a way in which you can clarify what has been said and get your team colleague to talk freely and in depth. Reflecting is useful in exploring the teacher's feelings. Reflecting calls for active listening, which enables you to pick up emotional overtones of what the other person is saying. Reflecting questions usually begin with: 'You feel they . . .?', 'You say you feel . . .?', 'You sound as if . . .?', 'You seem surprised . . .?', 'How do you feel . . .?', 'It must have been problematic . . .?', 'I get the feeling . . .?'

Hypothetical questions
These are quite useful for testing out ideas and opinions. An example might be: *'If we were to assume . . . what do think you would say?'*

Extending questions
Use these to invite further explanation and to prompt a further response, for example: *'How else could . . .?'*, *'Could you tell me more about . . .?'*

Comparative questions
You may find it helpful to use this type of question to compare a situation on a 'before' and 'after' basis, for example: *'What has it been like for you since . . .?'*, *'What difference has that experience made to your attitude towards . . .?'*

Linking questions
These questions are especially useful for picking up on things said earlier and linking them with something said more recently, for example: *'You mentioned earlier that . . . how would you deal with things now?'*

Try to avoid the following styles of questions, which are generally counter-productive:

Leading questions
These are occasionally 'loaded' questions, i.e. they have the answer implied in the question. These questions should be avoided because they suggest your personal views or feelings – even prejudices – which are not necessarily those of the other person. Examples might be: *'I assume that you . . .?'*, *'You wouldn't normally do that would you?'*, *'Don't you feel that . . .?'*

Multiple questions
These consist of a number of questions presented as a complete package. Not only are they confusing, but the other person will probably only answer one question, the one heard last. An example of this style of questions is: *'What was your main reason for . . . why did you . . . how do you like . . . and where was the . . .?'*

Confrontational question
Asking this kind of question is rarely advisable but can be used to check the values held by a colleague, for example: *'Can you really be that naive in allowing things to go that far before taking action?'*

Once you are aware of the types of questions and how they might be used, you may like to consider your patterns of questioning. Each of us learns or adopts different patterns of questioning, which deploy recall and process questions in different ways. The following list outlines the various patterns available to us.

- **Funnel pattern:** The questioning funnel is a useful idea for guiding the way you use questions to elicit information or gain commitment to action. When you adopt this pattern of questioning you tend to start with open questions and lead on to very specific ones. For example: *'Tell me about your previous role.' 'You say you did a lot with ICT.' 'What did you find that worked particularly well with the more able?'*

- **Pyramid pattern:** When using the pyramid pattern, the questioner starts with closed questions and then opens out. Pyramid questioning helps to concentrate the mind of the reviewee. For example: *'Did you make use of ICT in your last job?' 'What aspects did you find difficult?' 'How do you think we could persuade staff of the benefits of using ICT in their teaching?'*

- **Erratic pattern:** There is no evident pattern in the form of questioning but it is a style of questioning that is frequently adopted. Erratic questioning can cause confusion and stress. For example: *'How are you getting on with the new recording system? Incidentally, have I told you about the new computer software I've bought? Anyway, the recording system – what do you think?'*

Point for reflection

Having studied the above section on questioning skills, consider the following questions:

- Do I fall into the trap of believing all open questions to be 'good' and all closed questions to be 'bad'?
- Do I use complicated 'multiple' questions?
- Do I use 'leading' questions too often?
- Do I interrupt with another question before the first one has been answered?
- Do I make statements instead of using questions?
- Do I use an inappropriate tone of voice?
- Do I funnel my questions?

Listening skills

> *Listening in dialogue is listening more to meaning than to words ... In true listening we reach behind the words, see through them to find the person who is being revealed. Listening is a search to find the treasure of the true person, as revealed verbally and non-verbally. There is a semantic problem of course. The words have a different connotation for you than they do for me. Consequently, I can never tell you what you said but only what I heard. I will have to rephrase what you said and check it with you to make sure that what left your heart and mind arrived in my mind and heart intact and without distortion.*

(John Powell, quoted in Bolton, 1987)

Constructive questioning is of little value if it is not accompanied by active listening. It has been said that we hear with our ears and listen with our brains.

Table 9.6 Using the four basic communication skills

Skill	Listening	Speaking	Reading	Writing
Used	45%	30%	16%	9%
Taught	Least	Next least	Next most	Most

Good listening means more than just hearing. It means understanding well enough to enable interpretation, evaluation and appropriate reaction. Table 9.6 shows how much we use, and are taught, the four basic communication skills. It is interesting that the most used skill – listening – is, in general, the least taught!

Listening is a perfectly natural act for all of us but there are at least three main barriers to effective listening:

- selective attention – we decide whether we are going to listen or not;

- selective interpretation – we decide how we interpret the information, based on our perspectives or agenda; and

- selective retention – we decide what to remember, based on what we interpret as important.

Listening at a review meeting is a multi-functional activity because when we are listening we are also faced with interesting dilemmas. First, the speed at which we think. It is believed that, on average, a person talks at about 125 words per minute. The brain can think at speeds of up to 500 words per minute. What we tend to do is use this surplus capacity to judge, evaluate, compile responses or generally become distracted, while the other person is still speaking. Secondly, there are the problems caused by outside distractions of fatigue, discomfort, noise, movement, telephone calls, etc. It is difficult to concentrate on the other person's message if other unwanted messages keep intruding and super-imposing themselves.

To be a really good reviewer we need to listen actively – not passively. This means that we have to concentrate and focus, as well as let the other person know that we are listening. The key stages are:

- deciding to listen;
- listening neutrally – retaining information without interpretation;
- acknowledging – reflecting back what is said and felt;
- clarifying – statements or questions to show understanding of the implications ;
- summarizing – facts, situations, agreements, disagreements or actions;
- understanding; and
- considering a response – only possible after the other stages.

Remember that, to be a good team leader, you need to do at least twice as much listening as talking.

Point for reflection

How good a listener are you? Use the following activity to help you gauge your skill levels.

	usually	never
1. I make regular eye contact with the speaker.		
2. I interrupt often.		
3. I ask questions for clarification.		
4. I show concern by acknowledging feelings.		
5. I think about my reply while the other person is speaking.		
6. I restate or paraphrase some of the speaker's words to show that I understand.		
7. I jump to conclusions.		
8. I don't change the subject without warning.		
9. I am parental and answer with advice.		
10. I react non-verbally with a smile, nod, frown or a touch, if appropriate.		
11. I pay close attention and do not let my mind wander.		
12. I make up my mind before I have all of the information.		
13. I get easily frustrated when others cannot express themselves clearly.		
14. I am impatient.		
15. I finish other people's sentences.		

What have the outcomes of this activity revealed about the quality of your listening skills? What action might you now take to address the weaker aspects of your listening skills?

Feedback skills

See section on p. 155.

HOW DO I HANDLE PAUSES AND SILENCES?

Many find pauses and silences difficult to handle. Too often we are afraid to wait out the silence and we jump in to fill it with words. Use pauses and silences to your advantage because they allow you time to assimilate information, reflect and format a reply. The more complex the information, the longer the time required.

Point for reflection

It is easy during a meeting to become so concerned about what you want to say that listening stops in the real sense. Are you guilty of any of these listening shortcomings?

- making hasty judgements
- finishing other people's sentences
- showing impatience
- listening selectively
- daydreaming or letting your mind wander
- being easily distracted
- interrupting

HOW IMPORTANT IS BODY LANGUAGE/NON-VERBAL COMMUNICATION?

When you talk directly with people, as you will do in a performance review meeting, the meaning they take from what you say depends not only on the words you use but on other messages – body language – given by your facial expressions, the way you stand, the gestures you use, the movements you make and your tone of voice (Figure 9.3). So, as you see, a substantial part of what we say is communicated non-verbally, particularly if we are feeling nervous and are therefore incongruent, i.e. saying one thing while our body language says another. Positive non-verbal communication strategies include:

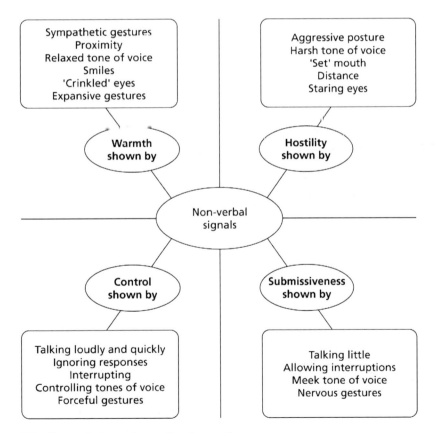

Figure 9.3 **Non-verbal signals creating impressions**

- smiling and looking welcoming;

- sitting so that you can see and be seen – avoid being behind a desk;

- having regular, comfortable eye contact;

- avoiding constant note-taking and distracting gestures;

- cultivating an open, interested and encouraging expression; and

- avoiding frowning if the person says something negative about themselves as this may inhibit disclosure.

Point for reflection

Body language messages can be read from facial expression – position of the head; posture; eye contact; body contact; and gestures. What messages would you get if, at your performance review meeting, your team leader did the following:

- **tilted his/her head to one side**
- **held his/her head down**
- **lent slightly towards you**
- **lent away from you**
- **placed his/her hands on the hips**
- **avoided eye contact with you**
- **put their arms around your shoulders**
- **nodded often following things you said**
- **shrugged their shoulders**
- **yawned**
- **covered their mouth with their hands and dropped their gaze**

HOW DO I MAKE NOTES AT THE REVIEW DISCUSSION AND STILL SHOW THAT I AM REALLY LISTENING?

There are good practical reasons for making notes during the review discussion. It can be difficult to remember everything that was discussed and agreed and yet, note-taking, if badly handled, can be very off-putting at the meeting. Always explain the purpose of your note-taking to the other person. You may find that they too wish to take notes. If so, encourage them to do so and, if necessary, ensure they have time to do so. It might be a good idea to say something like: 'That's an important point, let's note it down while we remember.' Try to avoid situations where:

- you are so busy taking notes that you forget to listen properly;

- you make the other person feel worried about the extent of your notes; and

- long silences are created while you write.

Limit your note-taking to:

- factual information gained during the discussion;

- new ideas for developing potential and augmenting existing competences;

- noting constructive suggestions made;

- action agreed/other people to be involved; and

- training opportunities agreed.

HOW DO I GIVE FEEDBACK IN A HELPFUL AND CONSTRUCTIVE WAY?

Giving relevant feedback, objectively and positively, is one of the key skills of conducting performance reviews. Throughout the review meeting, there will be a need to give feedback to the other person to ensure that they know your reaction either to what is being said or to proposals or suggestions that are being made. Some feedback will be verbal, while other feedback will be non-verbal. Constructive feedback increases self-awareness, provides options and encourages development, so it can be important to give and receive it. Feedback deals with the behaviours that individuals can change. According to Naisby (2002): 'Feedback is a mirror; reflecting back to the giver information about, and examples of, their behaviour and how this affects others. It also offers suggestions and advice.'

Giving positive feedback reinforces correct decisions, actions and behaviour. It helps build confidence and motivates staff to repeat what works. As the review meeting is about developing competence and skill, use language carefully when giving feedback. Select terms that are specific, concrete and behaviour-orientated. For example: 'It would help if you smiled a little more or looked at the particular child when you speak'. Where possible, choose positive words as opposed to those that smack of negativity. For example 'enhanced competence', 'development' or 'new skills' have a far more positive ring about them than 'problems', 'shortfall', and 'decline'. The review meeting is about future development, not just about past performance, so when we give feedback we should try to:

- provide it at the earliest opportunity, in an appropriate environment;

- introduce the subject under discussion on a note of praise wherever possible;

- identify positive behaviour using specific information and concrete, behavioural examples as evidence;

- ask and confirm the impact of the behaviour in order to help the teacher to see the benefits of the behaviour; and

- reinforce continued use of the behaviour.

And, be constantly aware that:

- feedback should be about specific, observable behaviour;

- perceptions, reactions and views should be presented as such, and not as facts;
- feedback should refer to the behaviour or outcomes being discussed, not the individual as a person or to their personality;
- in discussing difficult areas, in which there are established policies and procedures for achieving solutions, make suggestions about how these can help;
- when feedback has to be evaluative rather than purely descriptive, ensure that it is given in terms of established criteria, probable outcomes, or possible improvements as opposed to making judgements of 'good' and 'bad';
- feedback should be concerned with those things over which the person involved can exercise some control, and may include indicators of how the feedback can be used for improvement or planning alternative actions;
- terms which could produce emotional reactions in or raise the defences of the other person, should be avoided;
- if you encounter raised defences or emotional reactions, you should deal with those reactions rather than trying to convince, reason or supply additional information;
- feedback should be given in a manner which shows that you accept the other person as worthwhile;
- your non-verbal feedback supports the message of the words you use;
- you should be sensitive to the other person's reaction to your feedback;
- you should adapt your tone/language in feedback to the other person's reaction; and
- to be useful, feedback has to mean something and be acceptable to the other person.

Team leaders should also try to avoid:

- making statements of a general nature;
- making judgements;
- assuming that they know what the person meant to do ;
- making personality-type comments; and
- giving advice just because they want to give it.

HOW DO I GIVE CONSTRUCTIVE FEEDBACK IN NEGATIVE SITUATIONS?

Constructive feedback does not mean only positive feedback. Sometimes we have to give feedback when things are not going too well. We are often nervous about doing so because we do not want to harm relationships but negative feedback, given skilfully, is very important and extremely useful. To feed back positively and constructively we should try to:

- find something positive to acknowledge;

- introduce the subject under discussion;

- identify the behaviour being reviewed using specific examples and factual evidence;

- invite the reviewee to explore the impact of the behaviour and help them to realize the consequences of their behaviour;

- seek a solution – explore options and solutions; confirm right answers or offer suggestions; and

- agree the required solution and outcome – agree specifically the actions required; check and confirm commitment to action.

Point for reflection

In relation to what you have just read about giving feedback, ask yourself the following questions:

When giving feedback, do I:

- offer sufficient praise to the other person about things done well?
- make sure that any criticism offered is constructive?
- make promises that are unlikely to be kept?
- suggest training only where it is an appropriate solution rather than using it as a panacea or reward?
- make sure that my tone of voice/expression/body language reflect my words?
- give the other person time to think?

WHAT ELSE SHOULD I TAKE ACCOUNT OF WHEN COMMUNICATING WITH COLLEAGUES AT THE REVIEW?

Verbal communication

When communicating verbally we do so in order to:

- give information;

- seek information;

- express feelings;

- state opinions;

- establish and maintain relationships; and

- regulate social interaction.

The language we use, which is highly significant, has four main parameters:

- content – relates to the meaning of verbal language;
- structure – the way in which words are put together to form sentences;
- form – the way in which sounds are combined to form words; and
- use – the reasons why we use words.

The vocabulary, form and structure of the language we use varies from one social context to another e.g. formal and informal settings.

Paralinguistic features of communication

Communication also has some paralinguistic features. Words make up less than 10 per cent of the way a message is received when we communicate. Paralinguistics, or the way we say those words, accounts for about 40 per cent, and body language for the remaining 50 per cent. All of these things have an important effect on what the other person hears. The features of paralinguistic communication are shown in Table 9.7.

Proximity and contact

Proximity refers to the distance that people maintain between themselves during social encounters. Anyone intruding into the space tends to make us feel uncomfortable. There are cultural variations. However, this space has been classified into four zones, as shown in Table 9.8.

Table 9.7 Paralinguistic features of communication

Feature	What it conveys
Tone	The tone of voice used can sometimes suggest a different message from the words being used, i.e. giving mixed messages. The listener is left to decide which 'message' to believe, and it is usually the paralinguistic information (not the words used) that is accepted, as it reveals 'true' feelings.
Volume	We vary the volume of our voice depending on the situation and where and to whom we are speaking. Volume of speech can convey how a person is feeling, for example, loudness tends to be associated with anger and quietness with sadness or timidity. Volume is also closely linked with pitch and rate of speech.
Pitch	It is natural for people to use a range of frequencies during normal speech – their pitch range. Changes in these levels and ranges can convey information about the feelings and attitudes of the speaker. Pitch also has a major role in varying the meaning of what is being said. For example, by emphasizing key words in the same sentence the meaning can be changed.
Rate of speech	The rate at which we speak determines the clarity of what we say. Often, this rate is affected by the way we feel. For example, when we are angry, we tend to speak at a faster rate.

Table 9.8 **Proximity and contact**

Intimate	Personal	Social	Public
18" or 45 cm or less Only for those with whom we have a loving or intimate relationship.	18"–48" or 45 cm– 1.2 m When talking to friends in an informal situation.	4'–12' or 1.2–3.6 m When talking to strangers and acquaintances.	Greater than 12' or 3.6 m For talking to large groups.

HOW DO I MAINTAIN A GOOD RELATIONSHIP WITH A TEAM MEMBER TO WHOM I HAVE HAD TO GIVE NEGATIVE FEEDBACK?

Effective team leaders are those who are able to demonstrate relationship building and maintaining skills by conveying respect, genuineness and empathy. Having respect for another person, being genuine and being able to see things from their point of view, are crucial first steps. We then have to convey these beliefs by the ways in which we behave towards them (Table 9.9).

Table 9.9 **Relationship building skills**

What we convey	What it means	How we convey it
Respect	Making the other person feel valued, worthwhile, understood and prepared to trust the team leader	• listening actively • displaying warmth • being non-judgemental
Genuineness	Being ourselves, not hiding behind façades	• sharing feelings appropriately • talking about experiences appropriately • ensuring that verbal and non-verbal behaviour is consistent
Empathy	The ability to put ourselves in the shoes of the other person and see the world as s/he does – even if it is just for a moment	• reflecting feelings • talking about personal experiences appropriately

SUMMARY SELF-REVIEW

Spend a little time considering and then responding to the following review questions:

1. How thoroughly have I prepared for the performance review?

2. How thoroughly have I reviewed and updated the job description?

3. Have I held a pre-meeting with my team to brief them and help them prepare?

4. Have I asked 'open' questions?

5. Have I provided sufficient developmental feedback?

6. How well does the review provide an opportunity for teacher and team leader to reflect on the teachers' performance in a structured way?

7. How effectively did I make use of the review meeting to recognize achievements and to discuss areas for improvement and professional development?

8. How firmly focused are my reviews on exploring ways of raising performance and improving effectiveness?

9. How secure is my professional judgement about the overall effectiveness of team members in meeting individual objectives?

10. To what extent does my judgement take account of the stage my team colleague is at in his/her career?

11. Are the outcomes of the review meeting recorded appropriately in the review statement?

12. Are review statements written within the 10 days allowed?

13. Is there an agreed school format for the review statement? How well do I adhere to this?

14. How well have the review statements been completed?

15. How effective is the feedback I provide team members throughout the year as well as during formal review meetings?

16. How effective is my preparation for performance review meetings?

17. How well do I conduct review meetings with particular reference to:

   • creating the right atmosphere;

   • working to a clear structure;

   • using praise to get people to relax, to motivate and to provide them with encouragement;

   • letting the individual do most of the talking;

   • inviting self-appraisal;

   • discussing performance, not personality;

   • being positive;

   • not springing surprises on the individuals;

   • agreeing realistic and measurable objectives and an individual plan of action.

18. How effective has performance management been in developing teachers' skills and capabilities?

19. How effectively have I performed the role of coach?

20. Are objectives agreed in the key areas of pupil progress and developing and improving teachers' professional practice?

21. How confident am I that the agreed objectives are clear, concise, challenging, flexible and measurable?

22. How confident am I that the number of agreed objectives is appropriate for each team member?

23. How confident am I that team members understand what their objectives involve and how they will be reviewed?

24. Do teachers' objectives relate to the objectives in the school development plan?

25. Is a teacher's individual plan agreed with the team leader where responsibilities and objectives are clearly stated?

Action planning

Having spent some time reviewing your approach to conducting performance reviews, identify some actions that you might take to strengthen your current approach.

10 Coaching for Better Team Performance

Coaching is . . . about really paying attention to people – really believing them, really caring about them, really involving them.

(Peters and Austin, 1986)

INTRODUCTION

Downey (2001) illustrates the nature of the coaching process by pointing out that: 'in the sixteenth century, the English language defined coach as a carriage, a vehicle for conveying valued people from where they are to where they want to be'. Coaching has, for some time, been actively used in a business environment in the context of raising performance. The belief here is that the ability to raise the performance of staff and seek long-term goals for them to work towards is an important element of being a good team leader. This chapter helps you understand the purpose and benefits of coaching for yourself and the team, and shows you how to develop your coaching approach to get the best from your team and let you focus on bringing about improvements. The chapter addresses the following questions posed by team leaders:

- ➤ What is coaching?

- ➤ How does coaching benefit team members?

- ➤ How does coaching actually work?

- ➤ How well do I need to know my colleague to coach them well?

- ➤ What role is there for team leaders in coaching?

- ➤ What work situations may be conducive to a coaching approach?

- ➤ What makes a good coach?

- ➤ Are there different styles of coaching?

- ➤ How do I initiate a coaching session?

- ➤ How will I recognize a successful coaching relationship?

- ➤ Can I use coaching with the whole team rather than with individuals?

- ➤ Coaching seems to rely a great deal on trust – how can I build this trust with members of my team?

- ➤ How are knowledge, skills and behaviours applied in coaching situations?

- ➤ What are the characteristics of good listening within a coaching context?

➢ What hinders effective listening?

➢ In practical terms, how can team leaders manage the coaching relationship?

WHAT IS COACHING?

Everard (1998) refers to coaching as a central leadership and management tool: 'coaching . . . refers to the management activity of creating, by communication only, the climate, environment and context that empowers individuals and teams to generate results'. Coaching is a way of working with colleagues supportively in order to encourage them to develop personally and professionally. It is about helping them to improve beyond their present capability. It is, according to Megginson and Boydell (1979), 'a process in which a manager, through direct discussion and guided activity, helps a colleague to solve a problem, or to do a task better than would otherwise have been the case'. Through coaching, you can draw out the potential of your staff. Your team members will find this motivating because they will learn and be challenged by their work. Coaching is not therapy, counselling, or giving advice. It is also not technique-orientated or about rescuing unsatisfactory behaviour.

Point for reflection
In some way or another, we have all probably experienced coaching at some stage in our development, e.g. learning to ride a bike, drive a car, play a musical instrument, swim, learning different skills when taking up a new job. Think of a situation when you were coached or provided coaching for someone else.

- What are the key characteristics of successful coaching?
- What are the purposes of coaching?
- What are the benefits of coaching?
- Consider the knowledge, skills and behaviours necessary for an effective coaching relationship.

HOW DOES COACHING BENEFIT TEAM MEMBERS?

Coaching is a guided relationship process established with a team member in which both parties are accountable. The coaching process is forward-looking, change-orientated, and developmental. By coaching, team leaders release their own time, improve their team members' performance and enhance the quality of what goes on in the school. In short, coaching benefits team members by:

- helping them to improve their individual performance;

- providing a supportive working environment;

- encouraging them to value other people;

- improving communication;
- promoting the effectiveness of the team;
- ensuring the appropriate allocation of tasks and responsibilities;
- developing their leadership and managerial skills;
- expanding their range of skills, knowledge and insights in order to enhance their prospects for acquiring a different job;
- developing people for more senior jobs;
- increasing organizational effectiveness and efficiency; and
- enabling best use of resources.

According to McLeod (2000), a team that is mature in coaching terms is:

- open to challenge and is flexible;
- self-challenging; indeed its challenges are more internal than external;
- ahead of the competition;
- innovative;
- superbly supportive;
- involved in mentoring each other to new levels of performance;
- steeped in a 'we can do' philosophy; and
- committed to encouraging the best from themselves and their colleagues.

Point for reflection
Using McLeod's descriptions, how mature would you judge your team to be?

HOW DOES COACHING ACTUALLY WORK?

Successful coaching narrows the gap between an individual's or team's existing level of performance and the preferred one. In your coaching role you will be helping to develop team members by, together:

- appraising their performance;
- discussing the present situation;
- agreeing achievable goals;
- exploring new objectives; and
- agreeing a plan of action.

Coaching is an ongoing process. It can happen within a single session or over an extended series of sessions. It is important to remember that coaching is a

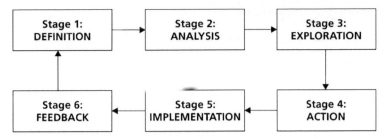

Figure 10.1 The six stages of a coaching cycle

continuous process – each new achievement forms a basis for future goals and achievements. For any single coaching goal, there is a cycle of six basic stages, as shown in Figure 10.1 and described in Table 10.1.

HOW WELL DO I NEED TO KNOW MY COLLEAGUES TO BE ABLE TO COACH THEM WELL?

It is not absolutely necessary to know everything about your colleague, or their work, to be able to coach them effectively. In fact, some excellent coaching takes place when the team leader is able to take a completely objective view of that staff member's goals without being distracted by extraneous detail. However, it is equally true that the coaching can be a richer process when the team leader is able to call upon his or her knowledge of the team member to illustrate points and recap on previous actions. The crucial thing is that you develop a coaching relationship in which your colleague:

Table 10.1 The coaching cycle described

Stage	Action
1. Definition	At this stage, you and the team agree the purpose of the coaching relationship. What will success look like? Will it be change in attitude, acquisition of new skills, greater confidence, etc?
2. Analysis	Stage 2 involves you in discussions with your team colleague regarding the current state of play. *'How are things at present?' 'What's working well – what isn't?'*
3. Exploration	The exploration stage is where both of you consider the available options in order that you can achieve the agreed goals. *What can we do about . . .?' 'What about trying . . .?'*
4. Action	This is where you outline and commit to a course of action. *'This is what we are going to do.'*
5. Implementation	This stage entails implementing the action agreed in Stage 4, with your help and support.
6. Feedback	At this point you discuss the learning that has taken place and how that can be added to the knowledge and understanding gained.

- learns from previous mistakes;

- identifies performance targets;

- takes responsibility for the action needed; and

- communicates what they think and feel.

Point for reflection

Think about each member of your team and try to respond to the following questions.

- How are they currently feeling about their work?
- What successes are giving them job satisfaction at the moment?
- What problems are causing them stress and anxiety?
- How are they progressing with their agreed performance management objectives?
- What are their career/personal development aspirations?
- How are they tackling new initiatives?
- How do they approach their own learning?
- Is anyone struggling unnecessarily?

WHAT ROLE IS THERE FOR TEAM LEADERS IN COACHING?

The role of the team leader in coaching is key to the development of a high performing team.

> The most successful teams are those who have demonstrated the greatest commitment to their people. They are the ones who have created the greatest sense of belonging. They have done most in-house to develop their people.
> (Bill Walsh, Head Coach San Francisco 49ers, quoted in Kerr, 1997)

Team leaders work with their colleagues to support and encourage them. Coaching is a way of working with colleagues to achieve precisely this. Coaches, like time leaders, combine a variety of skills e.g. listening, observing without judging, clarifying and agreeing action, in a way that helps team members to help themselves. Using coaching techniques, team leaders can more productively:

- support individual learning needs – by helping them tackle the tasks and the issues that concern them in their day-to-day job;

- encourage professional work-based development for the individual – it can be a learning experience for both team leader and team member via the opportunity to reflect on skills, knowledge and behaviour;

- involve team members in the learning process;

- help increase confidence, motivation and self-esteem;

- create development opportunities geared towards agreed standards, e.g. national standards;

- supply feedback leading to improved capability at work; and

- support for career development,

WHAT WORK SITUATIONS MAY BE CONDUCIVE TO A COACHING APPROACH?

Team leaders may find it beneficial to employ their coaching skills in the following circumstances:

- to orientate and induct a new team member;

- to teach a new job skill;

- to explain new procedures;

- to explain cultural norms of the school/team;

- to support a team member facing a new work experience;

- to help a team member to set objectives;

- to follow up a training session;

- to support a team member displaying low or moderate performance;

- to motivate a team member who needs reinforcement for good performance;

- to conduct formal or informal performance reviews; and

- to help a team member prepare to meet future career goals.

Point for reflection

Review the above work situations and, within the context of your specific role within the school, decide which ones might offer appropriate opportunities for coaching your colleagues. You may find it useful to consider how successfully you support members of your team currently. For example, how well do you support new staff joining the team, staff who are actively seeking career development, staff who are assuming new responsibilities within the team? Might coaching strengthen your existing approach?

WHAT MAKES A GOOD COACH?

Really effective coaches have to know themselves – they need to be self-aware and understand how they influence others. Heemsbergen (2000) suggests that coaching: '... is more about being than doing. It is more about essence than role. It comes from being authentic and congruent. The inner reality and the outer reality of the coach are not at odds with one another. Who the coach is and what the coach does are consistent.' Above all, coaches need to be:

- able to understand their personal feelings and keep them in check whatever the demands of the situation;

- emotionally resilient in the face of disappointment, adverse criticism or obstacles presented;

- able to remedy any errors and learn from the experience;

- able to maintain consistency in their moods and respectful towards those in the coaching relationship;

- honest with themselves and with others;

- able to demonstrate an unswerving commitment to continuous improvement; and

- able to focus on supporting the growth and development of the individuals in their care.

In the context of the school and supporting the work of the team, team leaders should aim to acquire and display the aspects of knowledge, understanding and behaviours and qualities outlined in Table 10.2.

Becoming an effective coach entails:

Creating a safe context in which to work

Team members will respond to your offers of support only if they feel safe in the context you create as their team leader. The things that you say and do are important in this respect. Let your colleagues know that the purpose of the coaching relationship is to support their overall development and effectiveness.

Really listening to what is being communicated

By fully listening to team members without interrupting or problem-solving, you set the stage that allows them to find their own answers. Hear the words and read the emotional content.

Asking probing and open-ended questions for real understanding

The aim is to explore opportunities and assist team members to challenge themselves. The key is to explore and facilitate, not tell or direct. Questions like 'Would you tell me more?', 'How is that so important to you?' and 'What would that look like?' are often part of helping team members to focus. Also helpful are behaviourally-based questions instead of hypothetical questions. For example, 'Tell me a time when you . . .?' rather than 'What would you do

Table 10.2 Knowledge, understanding, behaviours and qualities required by coaches

Knowledge	• context of the school • school improvement plan – priorities identified • range of data providing evidence and information • ethos and culture of the school • own knowledge and experience as classroom practitioner • own knowledge and experience as manager/team leader • job context of the individual being coached • opportunities/constraints for this individual • range of opportunities for professional development • access to professional development • resource implications
Understanding	• communication: active listening skills, reflective listening, open listening • appropriate questioning strategies • drawing out, recognizing and revealing feelings • giving feedback • negotiating and agreeing objectives • reviewing • ability to challenge • ability to confront • analytical skills • organizational skills • administrative skills • evaluative skills – ability to reflect and learn from experiences and • encourage others to do this
Behaviours and qualities	• integrity • honesty • sincerity • genuine interest and concern • trust • openness • understanding • empathy • willingness to share own skills • willingness to acknowledge own difficulties • willingness to challenge/set expectations • willingness to confront • willingness to reflect and learn from experiences

if . . .?' Vitally important to this questioning process is that you should be genuinely curious and in no way give the impression that you are judging, interrogating or manipulating your colleague.

Keeping the monkey off your back

The issues raised by team members are theirs. Adopting these issues by giving advice or solving the problem does not allow for team member development. Do not provide solutions – instead ask questions, explore options and facilitate the discovery of choices and possibilities. The aim is for the team member to find the answer that works best for them. Our answers work for us.

Giving and receiving useful feedback to aid development

Giving feedback that is goal-orientated and focused on future possibilities empowers individuals and creates intention. Immediate specific and focused feedback enables the development of an action plan. As coach, also be prepared to receive feedback. When it is given listen to it carefully, asking for specific examples. This will enable you to develop an action plan. Finally, check to ensure that you understood what was being said and follow through by acting on the feedback.

Developing an action plan and following up

The main goal is to have an agreement based on mutual accountability, with specific action steps to continue certain behaviours and use new ones. Together, you rehearse the future possibilities and plans, create agreement on the realism of the plans, and outline how to celebrate the achievement of outcomes. Follow-up should assist team members in staying on course with their plans.

ARE THERE DIFFERENT STYLES OF COACHING?

Because some of the people we work with will, at times, like clear direction and definite answers to their questions, while others will want to be involved in a dialogue about their development and objectives, it is important that team leaders are able to call upon appropriate styles of working. In fact, there is a spectrum of coaching styles ranging from 'push' at one extreme to 'pull' at the other (see Table 10.3).

To be able to apply the appropriate style, you have to understand what is going to motivate each individual to make the extra effort. The 'push' style is the most common form of coaching, especially in business and sport.

Table 10.3 **The different styles of coaching**

PULL ⇦	⇨ PUSH
When 'pulling', the coach:	When 'pushing', the coach:
• draws out strengths	• instructs
• listens more than he or she talks	• provides clear answers
• builds, e.g. *'Your idea about . . . is good, you might improve by . . .'*	• demonstrates skills
• tests understanding, e.g. *'What do you mean by that?*	• talks more than he or she listens
• summarizes, e.g. *'When we met today, John and I agreed that we should . . . using the same criteria that the team decided on.'*	• gives information, e.g. *'The group work didn't work at all well.'*
• seeks proposals, e.g. *'What can you do about . . . which was a slight problem today?'*	• proposes, e.g. *'I suggest that the best thing for you to do is . . .'*
• seeks information, e.g. *'What do we normally do when this happens?'*	

Point for reflection

Match your coaching skills to the motivation and skill levels of your team members. Who in your team is most likely to respond to a 'push' coaching style? Who will respond well to the 'pull' style? You may find it helpful to use the following criteria when gauging your team's 'will/skill' profile:

LOW WILL/LOW SKILL	LOW WILL/HIGH SKILL
HIGH WILL/LOW SKILL	HIGH WILL/HIGH SKILL

HOW DO I INITIATE A COACHING SESSION?

The first few steps you take in a coaching cycle lay the foundations for its likely success. Use the steps shown in Table 10.4 to help you become clear about how to initiate, structure, and follow up the session.

Point for reflection

Reflect on the following statements made by coaches. Which one(s) do you feel most strongly about? What are your reasons?

- *'Coaching off-site can encourage a more open discussion.'*
- *'A coaching session should never be interrupted.'*
- *'It is not necessary to say that you are going to "do coaching"'.*

HOW WILL I RECOGNIZE A SUCCESSFUL COACHING RELATIONSHIP?

A useful way of gauging the success of a coaching relationship is by using the **STAR** acronym – Situation, Task, Action, Result (Figure 10.2). Coaching needs to be identified as a learning opportunity. As a coach, the team leader is acting as:

- a role model – how to tackle problems and how to behave as a coach; and

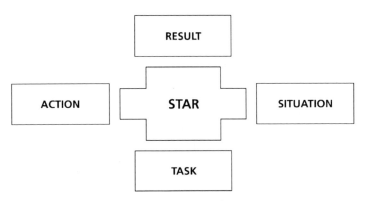

Figure 10.2 The STAR test for the coaching relationship

Table 10.4 Running a coaching session – from initiation to follow-up

Initiate a session

⇨

Look for opportunities	Clarify needs
Coaching can be both spontaneous and formal. It can be offered on a one-off basis or over a longer term over many sessions. It may be prompted by the team member or by the team leader. For example, a member of your team may approach you to discuss the possibility of promotion. Or, you may decide to initiate a coaching session when you notice a team member is having problems with an aspect of their teaching or personal organization. The crucial thing is to be ready to initiate coaching when you see an appropriate moment, or when requested by staff.	Whatever the situation, clarify the purpose of the session so that both parties know what they are doing, how they intend to do it and when coaching is going to work. If a member of your team raises an issue that you feel may be resolved through coaching, suggest that it would be helpful to have some time together to explore the issue. If, in your role as team leader, you have noticed a performance issue that needs attention, make it clear that you want to collaborate on finding a solution. In any case, state the benefits of a session and be clear about what you will each work on.

⇨

Start the session

⇨

Be positive	Clarify the issues	Agree the agenda
Set the tone for the session by choosing your first remarks carefully. Put your colleague at ease, for example, by conversing about unrelated matters, shared interests. Praise any achievements and draw particular attention to progress and work done well. This will convey positive interest and focus attention on performance. Try also to agree the length of the session so that you can plan a realistic amount of ground to cover.	You may have called the session in order to focus on career development, to talk about a new procedure, or to discuss a performance issue. Try to outline the reason for your interest – explain the issue or the problem. If your colleague acknowledges that the problem exists, it allows you to move on. If appropriate, it may be helpful to explain the consequences (for the school, the team) if the problem continues.	If the session has been initiated by the team member, take a little time to re-state your understanding of the reasons for the meeting. Clarify any points on which you are still unclear, using a range of 'open questions' (discussed in the previous chapter). Agree an agenda around the desired outcomes.

Shape the session

Define goals	Check reality	Discuss options	Agree timescales
Defining goals is at the heart of effective coaching. Goals not only provide a structure for the coaching session itself but also a clear focus for future action.	It is important for the coach to understand the reality of the situation as perceived by the staff member. This is where active listening is so important. Try to be attentive and supportive throughout.	Draw out ideas and solutions from your team colleague. See whether their strengths and past successes can be built upon to create new solutions. Praise their contribution whenever possible, but ensure that you are both clear about what needs to be achieved.	Once goals have been defined, reality checked and options explored, it is up to the team member to select the most useful options and plan the action needed. Ensure that there is commitment to this action within an agreed timescale, e.g. confer with a colleague, try a teaching technique.
Agree a goal for the meeting because this helps you to focus. Try to agree a goal that can be met in the time you have set aside. Check periodically whether you are making progress towards achieving the goals. If not, consider how to modify the session to bring about greater progress.	Some team members may view coaching as a chance to offload grumbles rather than focus on improving their performance. Try to let your colleague feel heard without allowing the session to be deflected from meeting its aim.	It is a good idea to try to identify and exploit colleagues' strengths and capabilities. Mobilizing these talents and capabilities in the search for new ways to achieve goals is very important.	
Create ideal goals by describing the end itself, not the means to an end. Try to agree goals that your colleague will be motivated to achieve. Once agreed, find practical ways of achieving the goal.	Controlling the flow of what is being said to you can be difficult. Listen carefully, but if you become overwhelmed with information, suggest a summary of what has been said. Pose a question that clarifies a point or leads on to a consideration of a possible option.	Discuss the difference between effective and ineffective performance. If for example, your colleague is having a problem handling a difficult staff member, invite him or her to think of an occasion when they saw them being handled successfully. This helps the person being coached to be reflective about personal performance.	

Table 10.4 Continued

Define goals	Check reality	Discuss options	Agree timescales
Use the mnemonic **SMART** to help you to set specific goals: Specific Measured Achievable Realistic Timed	During a coaching session, take note of voice, facial expressions and gestures. These may help you understand whether your colleague is focused, passive, confused, positive, etc.	Encourage your colleague to develop high, yet realistic, expectations.	

⇨

Take action

⇨   ⇨   ⇨

Set tasks	Reach agreement	Gauge commitment
Successful coaching sessions result in options which, in turn, form the basis for future action. The purpose of task-setting is to help the one being coached to reach the agreed goal. Tasks should match your colleague's competence and level of confidence yet, extend the person without overwhelming him or her. Agree the part you will play in supporting him or her.	To build the sense of ownership felt by the one being coached, try to agree – rather than set – tasks. Ensure agreement by summarizing the options you discussed, and select those that are most likely to succeed. Check for full understanding and total commitment.	A demanding action plan challenges the commitment of the one being coached as it may require significant change in his or her behaviour. Unless commitment is high, success is unlikely. Gauge the level of commitment by probing for levels of enthusiasm, e.g. observe non-verbal signs. Deal with remaining doubts.

⇨

Follow up the session

⇨

⇨

⇨

Follow-up sessions	Monitor change	Modify goals
Coaching, like any learning process, is ongoing. Keep up the momentum of learning by building in follow-up sessions where you can link work completed with the action plan. Arrange these sessions to coincide with the completion of key aspects of the action plan.	Concentrate on spotting small successes – they lead to bigger ones and will help increase momentum. Let your staff know that you are there for them to support, to acknowledge success and to praise.	Coaching requires that each member of the team is challenged fittingly in order to improve upon their previous best performance. Helping colleagues generate new performance goals is important.

- a facilitator of learning – by giving the opportunity for clear and explicit discussion of problems and issues.

CAN I USE COACHING WITH THE WHOLE TEAM RATHER THAN WITH INDIVIDUALS?

The coaching process can be highly valuable for supporting your team in achieving its goals. You may have to modify your coaching style but, ultimately, the process still relies upon the team's commitment to:

- defining goals;

- generating options; and

- taking responsibility for tasks.

The team's development plan, e.g. departmental plan, key stage plan, can be very useful in providing this level of detail.

COACHING SEEMS TO RELY A GREAT DEAL ON TRUST – HOW CAN I BUILD THIS TRUST WITH MEMBERS OF MY TEAM?

There is little doubt that, to be an effective coach, the team leader needs to build trusting relationships. With little or no trust, even the most technically correct system will not enable feedback and coaching to be effective. Trusting relationships can be achieved if team leaders pay attention to the following 'trust builders':

- clarity of communication – both orally and in writing;

- establishing clear and positive expectations – being clear about what is expected, forming expectations so that people feel positive and supported;

- listening – attending actively to what others say;

- openness – being willing to explore new possibilities and new experiences;

- admitting mistakes – showing a willingness to admit to mistakes you've made and making amends rather than maintaining an image of perfection and arrogance and denying responsibility for mistakes or placing blame on others;

- disclosing – being willing to share useful information even when it might make you vulnerable (for example, a mistake that taught a useful lesson);

- valuing – respecting the viewpoints, ideas and ideals of others; actually hearing what others say;

- involving others – drawing out the opinions, feelings, ideas, skills of others and asking for their help and participation;

- making and keeping commitments; honouring expectations – taking promises seriously and delivering on those made; offering to help move work forward; confirming who, what and when;

- sensitivity – being authentic and honest, 'walking like one talks', saying identical things to the other's face and behind the other's back; being straightforward versus 'playing games'; and

- technical competence – being respected as capable of doing the job well – skilful in some aspects.

Point for reflection

Success in coaching depends on trust. What does the term 'trust' mean for you? Think of someone whom you trust. What is it about that person that earns your trust?

HOW ARE KNOWLEDGE, SKILLS AND BEHAVIOURS APPLIED IN COACHING SITUATIONS?

Table 10.5 shows what skills and levels of knowledge are needed at the various stages of the coaching process and includes tips on what behaviours should be applied.

WHAT ARE THE CHARACTERISTICS OF GOOD LISTENING WITHIN A COACHING CONTEXT?

Focused listening is one of the most important skills for establishing such a relationship. It involves investing in understanding before being understood. Individuals may know exactly what they want to say. They may express themselves clearly but if the team leader understands differently, the individual will feel misunderstood and communication will break down. Crucially, effective listening involves:

- making appropriate eye contact;

- using non-verbal prompts, which encourage the person to continue speaking, e.g. nodding occasionally; using appropriate facial expressions, in response to the person's feelings rather than your own reactions to them; tolerating silence to communicate patience;

- sitting at an angle or adjacent to rather than opposite the person;

- adopting appropriate stance, e.g. open rather than folded arms;

- avoiding distractions, such as tapping pencils, etc.;

- focusing the discussion: 'Which is the most important thing that we've talked about in the last ten minutes?';

Table 10.5 **Knowledge, skills and behaviours applied in coaching situations**

Coaching process	Skills needed	Knowledge needed	Tips
Identify the gap/respond to requests	• Listening • Questioning • Reflecting • Gathering information • Observing	• Knowledge of the job and potential areas of difficulty. • Knowledge of the individual's job role.	• Make sure you validate all information against agreed levels of performance.
Consider learning styles and barriers	• Listening • Questioning • Reflecting • Gathering information	• Knowledge of potential learning options • Awareness of your learning style and how that may impact on a coaching activity.	• Use the learning styles questionnaire – it's fun and can provide valuable information.
Agree and note objectives	• Listening • Questioning • Objective setting and writing • Task and job analysis	• Principles of SMART objectives.	• Use action verbs, e.g. review, synthesize, reflect, analyse, to help produce SMART objectives. • Remember objectives need to reflect agreed performance levels.
Discuss and agree learning options	• Listening • Questioning • Reflecting • Gathering information • Matching learning options to learning styles.	• Awareness of a variety of learning options and how these relate to the potential coaching session.	• Try to encourage the learner to identify how the coaching session should run.

Consider the planning of the session and agree the plan	• Listening • Questioning • Time management • Resource management • Negotiation skills • Written communication	• Knowledge of resources available, people, materials and of job roles and responsibilities and working patterns. • Planning and preparing demonstrations, presentations and discussions.	• Ensure you make enough time for the session and remember to inform anyone else who may be affected.
Action the plan	• Listening • Reflecting • Questioning • Encouraging • Recording skills • Feedback skills	• How to analyse tasks. • How people learn. • What motivates individuals. • Subject knowledge.	• Remember to keep the session learner-centred.
Review the plan	• Listening • Reflecting • Questioning • Encouraging • Recording skills • Feedback skills	• Knowledge of the feedback process and how to encourage learner self-assessment.	• Review should be ongoing. • Provide options and choices and enable the learner to reflect on achievements as well as planning for the future.

- using verbal prompts such as 'um hum, ye-es, go on. I see. Can you tell me more about that . . .';

- using the 'playback' technique, i.e. repeat a key word – one word to avoid breaking the train of thought;

- asking questions to clarify meaning such as 'How do you feel about it? Can you give me an example? What does that mean to you?;

- paraphrasing what has been said to further discussion without interrupting thinking: 'So you felt very pleased with that, you . . .'; and

- summarizing what has been said to the satisfaction of the speaker.

WHAT HINDERS EFFECTIVE LISTENING?

A number of factors contribute to ineffective listening. Here are some to look out for:

- 'Open ears-closed mind' listening – jumping to conclusions about what the speaker will say, therefore adopting a closed mind because 'we will learn nothing new'.

- 'On-off listening'. This is where we are using the time to think about what we are going to say next, etc; when this happens we are not listening to what is being said.

- 'Glazed look' listening. We are looking at the speaker, but not listening because our minds are on other things.

- 'Red-flag' listening. We block out or interrupt the speaker because key words have engendered an emotional response.

- Trying 'obviously' to listen. Repeating facts, consequently missing new facts.

- Avoiding the issue. Not listening to or asking for clarification because the subject appears too difficult or complex.

- 'Matter over mind' listening. We have already decided on the outcome, therefore refuse to have own ideas and points of view challenged.

- Focusing on the subject instead of the speaker. Details and facts about an incident become more important than what people are saying about themselves. There is a danger here of missing key facts and speaker's expressions.

- Allowing external distractions, corridor noise, telephone, etc. to take over our attention.

Point for reflection

Think of a friend, a family member, or a professional colleague who displays the skills of effective listening. What does he or she actually do to demonstrate active listening? How does he or she make you feel when you are being listened to in this way? What have you learnt about your skills level in active listening?

IN PRACTICAL TERMS, HOW CAN TEAM LEADERS MANAGE THE COACHING RELATIONSHIP?

Table 10.6 sets out guidance on how you might manage the relationship you will need to establish before, during and after the coaching session.

Table 10.6 Managing the coaching relationship

Stage in relationship	What you can do
Before	<ul><li>allocate time and agree an agenda in advance to enable preparation</li><li>organize a venue which ensures privacy and is free of interruptions</li><li>prepare in advance, e.g. gather a range of evidence and data</li><li>analyse this to enable you to focus on areas for objectives</li><li>plan the structure of the interview</li><li>investigate possible sources of support</li><li>provide and seek information to improve overall effectiveness</li></ul>
During and after	<ul><li>help to identify strategies and solutions</li><li>offer support</li><li>identify other sources of support</li><li>give identified training and development needs to the staff development coordinator</li><li>plan and agree structures and processes for monitoring performance, e.g. lesson observation, work sampling, shadowing</li><li>evaluate the impact of any training undertaken</li><li>ensure ongoing regular review, feedback and coaching</li><li>ensure time to engage properly in the coaching process – particularly in seeing it as a reflective learning experience</li></ul>

Point for reflection

Below are some scenarios found in schools. Use them to judge the quality of your coaching skills.

Listening	Do you:
You are trying hard to meet a deadline and one of your team interrupts with a convoluted tale of a problem he has.	<ul><li>Listen in a distracted way while continuing with your task?</li><li>Stop what you are doing, invite him to sit down and tell you about the problem at his own pace and miss your deadline?</li><li>Stop what you are doing and give him your full attention for</li></ul>

<table>
<tr>
<td></td>
<td>five minutes? Then interrupt gently and arrange to meet him later so that you can give the problem fuller attention?
• Close the door before the starting the task to prevent such interruptions?</td>
</tr>
<tr>
<td>*Giving feedback*
A member of your team is working on a delegated task that you feel confident will stretch her but is within their abilities to complete.</td>
<td>Do you:
• Ask for daily written reports on how she is progressing?
• Let her get on with it and encourage her to ask if she has any problems?
• Ask regular, informal questions on specific aspects of the task to gauge progress?
• Ask her what would be appropriate intervals for holding review meetings?</td>
</tr>
<tr>
<td>*Communication*
You want to introduce a new planning and recording system for the work of the area. This will involve staff in making slight changes to the way they currently do things.</td>
<td>Do you:
• Send a memo/e-mail to everyone outlining the new method?
• Hold a meeting to discuss the new system and hand out the memo at the meeting?
• Pin a copy of the memo on the area noticeboard?
• Tell members of the team when you next bump into them?</td>
</tr>
<tr>
<td>*Handling poor performance*
A new staff member who has been in your team for less than 6 months is not settling well. During a lesson observation, you find that there is little evidence of planning and of meeting the needs of pupils with learning difficulties.</td>
<td>Do you:
• Give her a severe warning that, unless things improve, there will be serious consequences?
• Say nothing in the hope that she improves?
• Make time to have a meeting with her in order to review what happened, focusing on the action that is needed to improve?</td>
</tr>
</table>

SUMMARY SELF-REVIEW

Spend a little time considering and then responding to the following review questions:

1. On what basis do I really believe that my team members are capable of doing their jobs effectively and efficiently?

2. When I coach, is my focus on the past or on potential achievements?

3. When coaching, do I prefer to offer lots of input or do I prefer to listen to the opinion of others?

4. How prepared am I to receive negative feedback from team members?

5. How aware am I of any personal limitations when communicating?

6. How open and trustworthy am I viewed by team members?

7. How readily do I involve the team in making important decisions on our work?

8. Do I treat the team as partners or as subordinates? How do I know?

9. How do I ensure that my coaching sessions are free of interruptions and distractions?

10. How flexible am I in coaching sessions when, for example, changing focus from discussing goals to problem resolution?

11. How confident am I that team members can exercise responsibility when empowered to do so?

12. How capable am I of making links between the team's motivational needs and their goals?

13. How skillfully am I able to establish what is at the heart of my team members' concerns?

14. How aware am I of the non-verbal cues given off by my staff?

15. How firmly do I believe that every team member has underutilized strengths and talents?

16. How effectively do I summarize and reflect on what is said to help mutual understanding?

17. How effectively do I achieve a balance between asking open-ended as opposed to closed questions?

18. How confident am I at coaching colleagues who may not be members of my team?

19. How easy is it for me to acknowledge that there are different views about some issues?

20. How confident am I that my team members can find their own solution as a result of my coaching?

21. When giving feedback, how specific and constructive am I?

22. How do I set about securing colleagues' commitment to the task?

23. In what ways do I monitor agreements reached at coaching sessions?

24. How do I deal with any residual fears team members may have?

25. How good a role model am I when using the coaching approach?

26. If asked for advice, is it my natural style to offer it in the form of directions or in the form of suggestions?

Action planning

Having spent some time reviewing your approach to coaching, identify some actions that you might take to strengthen your current approach.

11 Developing an Action Research Culture within the Team

Research is a focused and systematic enquiry that goes beyond generally available knowledge to acquire specialised and detailed information, providing a basis for analysis and elucidatory comment on the topic of enquiry.

(Johnson, 1994)

INTRODUCTION

People carry out research for a number of reasons: some, to obtain a higher degree, e.g. masters and doctorates; others, to help them judge how effective their activities are and what can be done to bring about improvements. Traditional educational research has limited usefulness for classroom teachers. It often requires people to carry out specific research projects to the exclusion of their teaching. When educators talk about teacher research, or teaching as research they envision teachers extending their role to include critical reflection upon their teaching. Some examples of teaching as research include educators who wish to undertake research in their classrooms or schools for the purpose of improving teaching, to test educational theory, or to evaluate and implement an educational plan. Teacher researchers have adopted the label 'action research' to describe their particular approach to classroom research. This chapter provides guidance for team leaders who are seeking to develop an action research culture within their team in order to encourage improvement through reflective practice. It tries to do so by responding to the following key questions:

➤ What is action research?

➤ What do action researchers do?

➤ Why is research by practitioners important?

➤ What is the action research process?

➤ Won't staff resent the intrusion? Where does the time come from for carrying out the research?

➤ What skills do I need to carry out action research?

➤ How can I get the research under way? How will I know whether the project is manageable?

➤ How do I decide on my focus and identify my problem?

➤ How do I develop and implement a plan of action for my action research?

➤ Are there any ethical considerations I should be taking account of in my research?

➤ What should I take into consideration when collecting the data?

➤ What should I know about sampling, reliability, validity and bias?

➤ What techniques are there for dealing with data?

➤ What are the most effective techniques for data presentation and analysis?

➤ Once up and running, how do I keep track of the action research project?

➤ What exactly is a literature search? How do I plan a literature search?

➤ What is validation? Why is it important in the context of action research?

➤ How do I write up my action research? In what form should I present it?

WHAT IS ACTION RESEARCH?

There are many types of research but they all, '. . . are, or aim to be, planned, cautious, systematic, and reliable ways of finding out or deepening understanding' (Blaxter, Hughes and Tight, 1996). Action research is just one kind of research – a form of practitioner research – in which participants examine their own educational practice systematically and carefully using the techniques of research. Practitioner research simply means that the research is done by individuals themselves, or by teams of individuals, into their own practices. So, in the context of improving practice, there are two facets of action research: one is to bring about change and the other is to promote reflection among practitioners. It is based on the assumptions that:

● staff in schools work best on problems they have played a major part in identifying;

● staff become more effective when encouraged to examine and evaluate their own work and then consider ways of working more productively;

● staff help each other by working collaboratively; and

● working with colleagues helps staff in their professional development.

It could be argued that action research mimics the natural rhythm of the way we behave. For example, we do something – replace a fuse in an electrical item, say. We then check if it works as expected. If it doesn't, we analyse what happened and what we might do differently. If necessary we repeat the process. This is a natural cycle, the same one used in action research to achieve its twin outcomes of action (for example, change) and research (for example, understanding). The linking of the terms 'action' and 'research' highlights the key feature of action research in schools: trying out ideas in our place of work in order to improve and to increase our knowledge of teaching and learning.

Point for reflection

Using the following definitions of action research, identify the main characteristics of the action research approach:

- *'The fundamental aim of action research is to improve practice rather than to produce knowledge' (Elliott, 1991).*
- *'Action research is a form of self-reflective enquiry undertaken by participants in social (including educational) situations in order to improve the rationality and justice of (a) their own social or educational practices, (b) their understanding of these practices, and (c) the situations in which these practices are carried out' (Kemmis, 1988).*
- *'. . . action research does not have to be something carried out by a special group of people called researchers but is in fact what any practitioner could do as part of everyday practice, given certain conditions. Reflective practitioners are ipso facto researchers into their own practice' (Bryant, 1996).*

From these and other definitions it is possible to conclude that an action research approach can encourage team leaders and their teams to achieve the desirable personal outcomes highlighted in Table 11.1.

Table 11.1   Desirable personal outcomes of action research (adapted from Lomax, 2002)

Desirable personal outcome	How to achieve it
To be self-reflective	• by being thoughtful and by enquiring purposefully
To be self-critical	• by starting with open minds and not with prior knowledge of or bias about the outcomes • by showing willingness to having their ideas challenged
To be critical enquirers	• by challenging their existing assumptions, knowledge and practice
To improve	• by viewing themselves as educational professionals seeking improvements • by changing practice in line with identified values and goals • by adapting their current working practices if, and when, necessary • by reframing their current knowledge if, and when, necessary
To be rational	• by being committed to effective practice • by being committed to fairer practice
To bring about change	• by attempting to influence others via their school's practices and policies

WHAT DO ACTION RESEARCHERS DO?

Figure 11.1 sets out the key actions taken by action researchers.

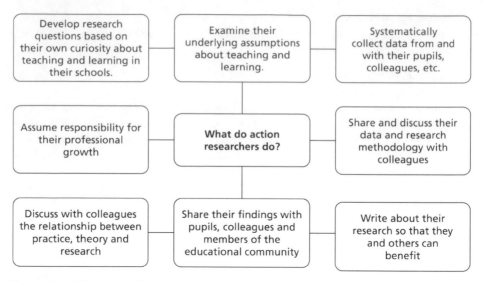

Figure 11.1 **What do action researchers do?**

WHY IS RESEARCH BY PRACTITIONERS IMPORTANT?

The case for encouraging staff in schools to engage in action research is a powerful one. This kind of research helps them to identify problems in their work and to find ways of overcoming them. Research can be undertaken either by individuals working on their own, or by a team working together. With team research, there is recognition that it can be a powerful aspect of a school improvement programme, providing ideas and evidence for individual, team and school development. A major advantage of team research is that colleagues can support each other through the notorious ups and downs of doing research. Team members can also contribute different points of view, resulting in a more thorough consideration of the research focus. The results of team research may also stand a better chance of being implemented simply because it demonstrates that a number of colleagues have been sufficiently concerned about an issue to try to do something about it. Well-planned and well-conducted action research can lead to:

Improved personal and professional development

An important aspect of action research is that the research should be educational and an enquiry into what we do. When you ask the question, 'How do I improve what I am doing?', the response will aid self-development. Self-development is inherent in the notion of a professional, and integral to the concept of professionalism. Self-development, through action research, is an extension of professional work, not an addition to it. It utilizes the experience of teachers and all who work in schools.

Better professional practice

Many staff in schools already carry out informal, personal enquiry related to their professional practice – they often reflect on their practice and modify things in the light of what they learn. Action research takes matters a little further and focuses on praxis rather than just practice.

> Praxis is informed, committed action that gives rise to knowledge rather than just successful action. It is informed because other people's views are taken into account. It is committed and intentional in terms of values that have been examined and can be argued. It leads to knowledge from and about educational practice.
>
> (McNiff, Lomax and Whitehead, 1996)

Improvements within the team and the school

The whole point of carrying out research is to find out something that we did not already know. That is, we are trying to add to our existing knowledge base by seeking explanations, descriptions, interpretations and knowledge. In this way, research contributes to our knowledge and the dissemination of research spreads that knowledge further.

WHAT IS THE ACTION RESEARCH PROCESS?

The processes of action research have been described in many ways by a variety of writers. Although various models exist which attempt to describe the action research process there does appear to be agreement among researchers that the process tends to operate in cycles. For example, Kemmis and McTaggart (1982) have developed a simple model representing the cyclical nature of the typical action research process, where each cycle has four steps: **plan**, **act**, **observe**, **reflect**. Such a representation is helpful in that it reflects the sometimes untidy world of action research – making plans, doing, undoing, making new plans, making mistakes, reflecting, modifying . . . – an untidy process represented in Figure 11.2.

WON'T STAFF RESENT THE INTRUSION? WHERE DOES THE TIME COME FROM FOR CARRYING OUT THE RESEARCH?

Elliott (1991) makes the point that where teachers viewed observers as researchers they were prepared to accept comment and tolerate loss of self-esteem. This loss of self-esteem was tolerated even more when they viewed themselves as action researchers. As their toleration levels rose, the more open they became to student feedback. Glatthorn (1990) observed that teachers participating in action research:

> . . . were more self-assured and willing to change and became better documenters of what took place in their classrooms. The teachers changed in their focus from teaching pupils to finding out what their pupils knew and helping them to learn; they asked more questions, listened more and saw pupil concerns as legitimate.

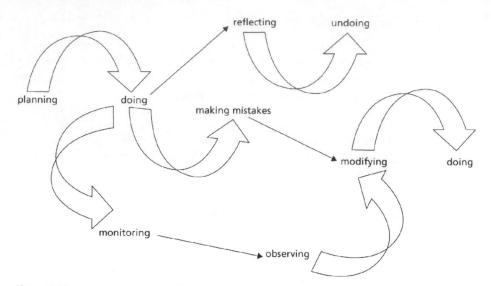

Figure 11.2 **A representation of the action research cycle**

Most people would agree that units of at least a whole day are preferable to allocating, say, an hour here or an hour there. This will give quality time for working and writing and the reflection so essential to the research process. Of course, this is not at all easy in schools, so often one has to settle for much shorter periods of time. One of the most crucial parts of planning a research project is to list and schedule all the tasks that need to be undertaken. Once done, the next job is to estimate a period of time for the completion of each task and schedule the list into a logical, sequential order. You now start to obtain a picture of your project and, with support, will be able to apportion tasks for yourself and members of the team.

WHAT SKILLS DO I NEED TO CARRY OUT ACTION RESEARCH?

Given the nature of action research, it is likely that you will need to be able to work with a range of others. You are likely to be working with:

- *participants in the research* – these are probably colleagues, students and anyone else who is going to be part of your research. You will rely heavily on these people and ensuring that they are fully in the picture and content about their role is an important skill to have. You can do this by:
  – explaining their role in providing data and evidence of changed practice;
  – respecting issues of access and confidentiality when the need arises;
  – inviting their comments on how things are going; and, of course,
  – thanking them.

- *critical friends* – these are people you are working with on the project. They could be members of the team, a tutor from a higher education establishment, an LEA adviser. Negotiating the ground rules of this relationship is important, if you are to secure meaningful feedback and overall support.

Each of the above is an invaluable resource and you need to display a range of interpersonal skills in order to build and maintain good relations. These skills, which include the following, are dealt with in other sections of the book:

- listening (including body language);

- planning (including target-setting);

- negotiation (including handling conflict);

- management (including managing meetings); and

- communication (including the use of appropriate language for different audiences).

HOW CAN I GET THE RESEARCH UNDER WAY? HOW WILL I KNOW WHETHER THE PROJECT IS MANAGEABLE?

Before making a start, think for a moment about how you are going to tackle the *whole* research project – assess realistically 'where' you are, 'what' you hope to achieve, and 'how' you think you might get there. Successful research relies on being clear in your own mind about:

- *What* you want to research.

- *Why* you want to research it.

- *How* you are going to research it.

Point for reflection
As a way of getting started, individually, and/or when working with your team, respond to the following 'starting point' statements:

- *'I would like to improve . . .'*
- *'I am baffled by . . .'*
- *'Some people are unhappy about . . .'*
- *'I'm really curious about . . .'*
- *'I want to learn more about . . .'*
- *'An idea I would like to try out with my class is . . .'*
- *'Something I think would really make a difference is . . .'*
- *'I would like to change . . .'*
- *'An area I'm particularly interested in is . . .'*

Several authors have provided models to describe the phases of action research. For example, Bassey (1998) sets out an eight-stage model of action research. These stages are shown in Table 11.2.

Table 11.2 Bassey's eight stages of action research

Stage	What you need to do	Questions to help you do it
Stage 1	*Define the inquiry*	• What is the issue of concern? • What research questions are we asking? • Who will be involved? • Where and when will it happen?
Stage 2	*Describe the educational situation*	• What are we required to do here? • What are we trying to do here? • What thinking underpins what we are doing?
Stage 3	*Collect evaluative data and analyse it*	• What is happening in this educational situation now as understood by the various participants? • Using research methods, what can we find out about it?
Stage 4	*Review the data and look for contradictions*	• What contradictions are there between what we would like to happen and what seems to happen?
Stage 5	*Tackle the contradiction by introducing change*	• By reflecting critically and creatively on the contradictions, what change can we introduce which we think is likely to be beneficial?
Stage 6	*Monitor the change*	• What happens day by day when the change is introduced?
Stage 7	*Analyse evaluative data about the change*	• What is happening to this educational situation now – as understood by the various participants – as a result of the changes introduced? • Using research methods what can we find out about it?
Stage 8	*Review the change and decide what to do next*	• Was the change worthwhile? • Are we going to continue it in the future? • What are we going to do next? • Is the change sufficient?

Source: Bassey, 1998

An alternative five-phase model is shown in Table 11.3 that offers practical suggestions for the action research process.

HOW DO I DECIDE ON MY FOCUS AND IDENTIFY MY PROBLEM?

You probably already have a number of ideas for your research, but the chances are that you will need to narrow them down so that you focus on something that is both interesting and manageable. There are at least five factors to bear in mind when identifying your focus. They are:

• **Your school context** – You are likely to be carrying out this research because you have some form of educational concern. This concern may have been identified by your school, or it may be one that you have identified for the school, or is one that has arisen directly from your own practice, e.g. a concern about children's attitudes to their own writing and that of their peers.

Table 11.3 **A five-phase model for action research planning**

Phase	What you need to do	Questions to help you do it
Phase 1	*Decide on a focus or identify the problem*	• What are my/our *broad* interests in teaching and learning? • What are my/our *specific* interests? • Is what I/we have chosen an important and practical problem? • Why do I/we want to do it? • Is the enquiry worth my/our time and effort? • Is this something that could be beneficial to me/us/ pupils, etc? • Have I/we stated the problem/issue clearly and in the form of a research question? • Is the question broad enough to allow for a range of insights and findings? • Is the enquiry feasible within the time-frame and my/our daily work?
Phase 2	*Develop a plan of action*	• Will I/we develop and implement a new strategy or approach to address the question? If so, what will it be? • Will I/we focus our study on existing practices? If so, which particular ones? • What is an appropriate time-frame for what I am/we are trying to accomplish?
Phase 3	*Collect Data*	• What types of data should I/we try to collect in order to answer the question? • How will I/we ensure that I/we have multiple perspectives? • What resources exist and what information from others might be useful in helping me/us to frame the question, decide on types of data to collect, or to help me/us in interpreting the findings?
Phase 4	*Analyse the data*	• What can I/we learn from the data? What patterns, insights and new understandings can I/we find? • What meaning do these patterns, insights and new understandings have for my/our practice? for the pupils?
Phase 5	*Plan for future action*	• What will I/we do differently in the classroom as a result of this study? • What might I/we recommend to others? • How will I/we write about what has been learned so that the findings will be useful to others?

- **Critical incidents** – You may find it helpful at this early stage to reflect on past and recent experiences that have had some impact on how you see yourself in your role, or the situation you work in. These critical incidents are a part of every reflective teacher's normal experience.

- **Purposes and audiences for your work** – As part of your planning, you need to think carefully about your own motives for wanting to initiate an enquiry. You need toconsider who else, in addition to yourself, is likely to be affected by any changes that result. You also need to think about the possible outcomes of the research and of any changes it might lead to. This is important if you wish to persuade others of the need for change.

- **Colleagues and friends** – Try not to overlook the potential contribution of colleagues and friends to your research. They can help by offering their views on what you propose to do; by telling you about what has happened in the past and which may affect how you decide to approach things; by giving you new ideas; by offering or agreeing to play a part in the research; and by providing moral and personal support.

- **Published materials and other resources** – There is no expectation that you will undertake an exhaustive survey of the literature associated with your chosen focus. However, do bear in mind that some reading of relevant materials, e.g. journals, books, can influence your research in several ways. They can help you choose and narrow your focus by giving you ideas of what other researchers are doing and have done; help you justify and explain better what you want to do and why; as well as helping you increase your knowledge of the topic area you are interested in.

When you have considered each of these, you should be in a position to draft two or three research questions (*specific* questions that you would like your research to answer). The research question is the backbone of research. Designing research entails formulating questions to be explored, developed and addressed through the research. Research questions should be distinguished from questions that you might include in a questionnaire or interview. Research questions stem from your research focus and are vital because they steer you towards the kinds of information you need and the way you should collect and analyse it. A research question is one that:

- makes explicit the precise area of investigation;

- identifies the specific aspects which are of concern;

- guides the researcher towards the kind of data which will inform the research issues; and

- is open-ended.

(adapted from Lewis and Munn, 1987)

Point for reflection

What are the characteristics of well-designed research questions? Why are they so crucial to the research? Write down the key questions that your research project seeks to address. Begin each one with a questioning word like 'how', 'who', 'what', 'when' or 'why'. Which of these questions is the most central to your research?

Table 11.4 Example of an outline research timetable proposal

Preparation	Discuss plans with headteacher and other staff Arrange times for interviews and observations. Draft and pilot: Interview schedule for staff interviews Observation schedule to observe lessons
Week 1	Observation schedule to observe individual pupils Timetable for collecting information (6 weeks) Check arrangements for interviews and observations
Week 2	Select individual children to observe (in consultation with staff) Interview headteacher and write report.
Week 3	Carry out first individual observations of selected children Interview 2 members of staff and write reports
Week 4	Interview 2 more members of staff and write up reports First classroom observation and interview with sample of pupils
Week 5	Interview 2 remaining members of staff and write up reports Second classroom observation and interview with sample of pupils
Week 6	Final classroom observation and interview with sample of pupils
Week 7	Second set of observations of individual children Write up summary of this and comparison with earlier observations

HOW DO I DEVELOP AND IMPLEMENT A PLAN OF ACTION FOR MY ACTION RESEARCH?

After the problem is identified and the research questions formulated, it is time to develop a plan of action to improve on the present situation. There is a need for a plan detailing who is going to do what, when it has to be completed, etc. The example in Table 11.4 provides such an outline plan. It is broad at this stage but provides you with the outline that you need. The full plan would probably include greater levels of detail, including:

- the group of people you intend to work with;

- the names of your critical friends; and

- your validating group.

ARE THERE ANY ETHICAL CONSIDERATIONS I SHOULD BE TAKING ACCOUNT OF IN MY RESEARCH?

The ethical considerations of your research may not be so significant, but nevertheless a fundamental principle of research is that you should be aware of the implications of your work. It is clear that data gathering activities will involve practitioners in new sets of relationships and it is necessary to ensure that the activities are compatible with other professional responsibilities. You are not like external researchers who may not dare or have to show their faces in an institution again! Set out in Table 11.5 are key ethical considerations for practitioner researchers.

Point for reflection

List the access and ethical issues that are likely to arise in your research project. Use Table 11.5 as a checklist.

Table 11.5 Ethical considerations for practitioner research (adapted from Kemmis and McTaggart (1982)

Ethical considerations	How to achieve them
Observe protocol	Ensure that the relevant people, committees and authorities have been consulted, informed and that the necessary permission and approval has been obtained.
Involve participants	Encourage others who have a stake in the improvement you envisage to influence the nature of the work.
Negotiate with those affected	Your work should take account of the responsibilities and wishes of others.
Report progress	Keep the work visible and be open to suggestions so that unforeseen and unseen consequences can be kept in mind.
Obtain explicit approval before you observe	This is particularly true of the professional colleagues you observe. The observations of your pupils falls outside this requirement provided that your aim is to improve teaching and learning.
Obtain explicit approval before you examine documentation	You should only take copies if you have obtained specific permission to do so.
Negotiate descriptions of people's work	Always allow your accounts to be challenged on the grounds of fairness, relevance and accuracy.
Negotiate accounts of others' points of view	Always allow those involved in interviews, meetings and written exchanges to request amendments that enhance fairness, relevance and accuracy.
Obtain explicit approval for using quotations	This includes verbatim transcripts, attributed observations, excerpts of audio- and video-recordings, judgements, conclusions or recommendations in reports (written or to meetings).
Negotiate reports for various levels of release	Bear in mind that different audiences require different kinds of reports, e.g. informal verbal, journal article, newsletter to parents.
Accept responsibility for maintaining confidentiality	Abide by any commitments you make to people to respect confidentiality.
Retain the right to report your work	As long as your accounts are viewed as being fair, accurate and relevant; do not expose or embarrass those involved, they should not be subject to veto.
Make your principles of procedure binding and known	Ensure that everyone involved in your research project agrees to the guiding principles before the work begins.

WHAT SHOULD I TAKE INTO CONSIDERATION WHEN COLLECTING THE DATA?

Once you have formulated your research questions you then need to consider which data collection method(s) will best inform your issue. Asking the right questions is the key skill in effective data collection. You and your team might find it helpful to use the checklist in Table 11.6 in relation to data collection.

Table 11.6 Considerations when collecting data

WHY *are we collecting this data?*	• What are we hoping to learn from the data? • What are we hoping to learn from using this particular data collection strategy? • Is there a match between what we hope to learn and the method we choose?
WHAT *exactly are we collecting?*	• What different sources of data will allow us to learn best about this topic? • What previously existing data can we use? • How much data do we need in order to really learn about this topic?
WHERE *are we going to collect the data and for how long?*	• What are the limitations to collecting the data? • What support systems need to be in place to allow for the data collection to occur? • In what ways might we build data collection into the normal activities of the classroom/school?
WHEN *are we going to collect the data and for how long?*	• Have we built into the plan data collection at more than one point in time? • What strategies can we use to easily observe and record data during lessons? • Where will the time come from to gather and record data using the strategies we have selected?
WHO *is going to collect the data?*	• To what extent can students generate any data? • How feasible is it for a colleague or a student teacher to assist with data collection? • What can I do without it being too overwhelming?
HOW *will data be collected and displayed?*	• How will I collect and display the data – qualitative or quantitative? • How will we set about analysing the data? • To whom will we present what we have learned?

WHAT SHOULD I KNOW ABOUT SAMPLING, RELIABILITY, VALIDITY AND BIAS?

Sampling

When undertaking action research in your team leadership role, you are likely to want to find out something about, or seek information from, particular categories of people, such as parents, school leavers, newly qualified teachers, or pupils. A 'population' consists of all possible people who fall into a particular category. Populations can be large, e.g. all school leavers within an LEA's secondary schools, or they can be small, e.g. the number of children undertaking national tests at KS1 in a small rural primary school. A 'sample' is a smaller number of individuals drawn from the total population and which is viewed as truly representative of that population.

Reliability

Research is said to be 'reliable' if it means that you can be confident that nearly identical conclusions would be reached if it were repeated at a different time, either by yourself or by someone else.

Validity

Although you may have taken great care to ensure that your research methods are reliable, it is not always the case that they will give you true, or 'valid', information concerning your choice of topic or issue. An example of this is when an interviewee is trying to please the interviewer by giving acceptable rather than honest responses. In other words, the information you are gathering fails to provide a valid reflection of people's opinions on the topic in question.

Bias

Bias means unfairly favouring one thing at the expense of another. It is an error that arises when we allow our own values, perceptions and expectations to influence the way in which we conduct our research. Bias can exert an effect at a number of different stages: for example, in the design of questionnaires or interview schedules; in the choice of children chosen to observe or test; in the choice of people you decide to interview, etc.

Point for reflection

With your action research project in mind, spend a little time considering issues of *sampling, reliability, validity* and *bias* that might arise.

WHAT TECHNIQUES ARE THERE FOR DEALING WITH DATA?

There are a number of techniques available for dealing with data (Table 11.7). It may be obvious, but the crucial thing is selecting the most appropriate one for your specific purpose. In respect of each data collection instrument available to you, consider:

- What are the strengths of each instrument?
- Which is the most 'do-able'?
- What constraints does each method present?
- How might the data collected be analysed?
- Do I have the skills needed to use the instrument?

Table 11.7 Data collection instruments

Collection methods	Advantages of method	Limitations of method
Diaries and logs written by teachers, students, parents, class groups	• Enables you to gain information about events you cannot observe. • Can be used flexibly.	• You may get different amounts and types of information from respondents. • Can be time-consuming to analyse.
Individual interviews with students, parents, teachers	• Does not run the risk of low response rate. • Allows you to probe particular issues in depth. • Likely to generate a lot of information. • Interviewer can pick up non-verbal cues. • People are easier to engage in an interview than by using a questionnaire.	• Takes time to set up and carry out. • Respondents may be affected by their perceptions of you and your research, and what responses they feel are appropriate. • Takes time to write up and analyse. • The responses can colour the interviewer's interpretation. • It is subjective – the reliability and validity depend on the quality of the interviewer.
Group interviews with teachers, parents, students	• More economical on time than several individual interviews. • Some respondents may prefer to be interviewed as a group. • May allow you to 'brain-storm' and explore ideas.	• It may be hard to manage a group discussion. • Respondents will be affected by others present in the interview. • Note-taking may not be easy. Writing up notes and analysis is relatively time-consuming.
Questionnaires (posted/ handed out) of attitudes, opinions, preferences, information	• Questionnaires do not take much time to administer, so useful for a large sample. • Everyone is asked the same questions. • Can be designed so that analysis is relatively simple.	• Response rate may be low and you could get a biased sample. • Danger of differing interpretations of the same questions – respondents cannot ask for explanations. • People's preferred responses may not be allowed for in your questionnaire.

Table 11.7 Continued

Collection methods	Advantages of method	Limitations of method
Questionnaires in situ of attitudes, opinions, preferences, information	• Takes less time to administer than individual interviews. • Higher response rate than postal questionnaires. • If need be, you can ask others to administer the questionnaire.	• Less flexible than individual interviews. • If you are not present while the questionnaire is administered response may be affected by something you are not aware of.
Documents other than classroom resources	• Gives access to information you can not find more directly. • May provide a particular viewpoint.	• Will inevitably provide a partial account. • May be biased.
Published facts and figures	• Provides numerical information – may provide a context for your own work. • Allows you to make comparisons between different contexts or different groups of people.	• Not always easy to use – often contain too much information that you need to select from and may not contain exactly the information you want. • Information may be misleading. Need to check basis of statistics (how collected; from what sources; what is included and what is not).
Classroom resources, e.g. videotapes, audiotapes	• Provides information on what is available for children to use – characteristics of resources.	• Cannot tell you how resources are used, or how responded to by pupils – needs to be supplemented by other sources of evidence.

Recollections	• Allows you to reflect after the event on part of the school day, or a meeting. You are likely to recall episodes that stand out. • Does not require any special arrangements for the observation. • Interferes very little with normal teaching or participation in a meeting. • Because it can be fitted in with everyday work, you may be able to carry out more extensive observations.	• There is a danger of unintended bias, exacerbated if you rely on recollections. • You cannot go back and check on any observations you are not sure of. • You will not be able to remember events in detail. • On any occasion, you will collect less information than someone recording at the time.
Observations of lessons, groups, demonstrations, discussions, interactions	• Allows you to observe points of interest as they occur. You can observe across a whole lesson/meeting or at selected intervals. • Requires preparation. • On any occasion, you will be able to make fuller observations than someone relying on recollections. • May be carried out in your lesson by a colleague or a pupil. • You can observe in a colleague's lesson.	• You only have a short time to decide what to record. • You cannot go back and check your observations afterwards. • You cannot do as detailed an analysis as would be possible with an audio- or video-recording. • It is difficult to carry out while teaching or taking an active part in a discussion or activity. • You need a relationship based on trust – and you may still be intrusive. Pupils may interrupt and ask for help.
Children's work e.g. student portfolios, photographs, tapes	• Can provide partial evidence of how your teaching has gone, or of pupils' knowledge and/or understanding. • Data can be collected by someone else. • You can return to, and reconsider, the evidence, and share interpretations with a colleague/pupils.	• Focuses on product of work – you may want additional evidence on process. • Work may be hard to interpret if you don't know the context in which it was produced. • Extensive scrutiny of children's work is time-consuming.

Following on from an earlier section in this chapter, it is important that the data collection instrument is both *valid* and *reliable*. *Validity* ensures that the data collected is relevant to the research. *Reliability* is the extent to which an instrument provides consistent results, if applied more than once to the same sample, under standard conditions.

WHAT ARE THE MOST EFFECTIVE TECHNIQUES FOR DATA PRESENTATION AND ANALYSIS?

Data analysis, along with data collection, is the real essence of the research process. Once all the hard work of data collection has been completed it is time to look for patterns and meaning and ordering across the complete data set. This could form the basis of explanations, new hypotheses and even theories. Data can be used in two ways: *descriptively* or *analytically*. In your research, whether the data is *qualitative* or *quantitative*, the important thing is to move from *description* to *explanation/theory* and then to *action/recommendation*. The following guidelines may help the process of analysing your data:

- Design a systematic approach to analyse your data. This may develop as you become more comfortable with what you are learning.

- Don't be afraid to let the data influence what you are learning as you go deeper with your analysis.

- Look for themes and patterns to emerge. Key words and phrases can trigger these. Look for those unique ideas that you had not considered which may influence your thinking.

- Make sure that you are organizing your data based on what you are learning. Include data that does not necessarily reflect change or growth. All of this is part of the learning experience and can still inform practice.

- Go through the data several times. New ideas will occur to you with a fresh perspective.

- Think about creating visual images of what you are learning. For example, a grid, an ideas map, a chart or some visual metaphor are all possibilities to help make sense of the data and display a powerful presentation of your ideas.

- Write lots of notes to yourself as you are sorting. This kind of reflection will help you as you step back and try to look at the big picture.

- Share your findings with a colleague. Do new questions emerge from the discussion?

- Let the data influence you. Jot down ideas for actions you will take as a result of what you are learning.

Point for reflection

Evaluate the following action research plan. What are its main strengths? In what ways might it be improved? In arriving at answers to the questions, what criteria did you have in mind?

Title of project	Managing the Implementation of Lesson Observation
Project aims	• To introduce lesson observations to enable sharing of good practice. • To survey current practice in lesson observation within the team. • To gauge team member attitudes towards lesson observation. • To evaluate the effectiveness of lesson observation as a tool for sharing good practice and extending professional development.
Key questions to be researched	• What is the extent and nature of lesson observations taking place currently? • For what purposes are the observations used at present? • What attitudes do (a) users and (b) non-users of lesson observation hold towards this form of professional development? • What constitutes an effective plan for using lesson observation? • How did the plan work out in practice? (intended and unintended outcomes)
Sources of data and methods of investigation	**Phase 1:** • Questionnaire survey of a sample of users and non-users of the process. • Selected interviews plus possible observation of current lesson observation process. **Phase 2:** • Team meeting minutes and planning documents. • Interviews with team members about their perceptions of: – the initiative – my performance as team leader in implementing it. • Record of amount of lesson observation conducted as a result of the initiative. • Team discussion about the impact of teaching and learning.

ONCE UP AND RUNNING, HOW DO I KEEP TRACK OF THE ACTION RESEARCH PROJECT?

At this point, it is probably worth emphasizing the 'action' component within action research; action that:

- you are committed to you because of your personal and professional values;

- is informed by your own professional knowledge and experience; and

- is intentional.

Keeping track of (monitoring) the action involves the following operations:

- gathering data about the action so that it provides an accurate record of what took place;

- interpreting the data collected in order to provide a tentative explanation of what took place; and

- evaluating what has been done so that amendments can be put in place.

Keeping track of (monitoring) the action will entail data collection. This data will be used as a basis to reflect and evaluate what has taken place before planning future action.

WHAT EXACTLY IS A LITERATURE REVIEW? HOW DO I PLAN A LITERATURE SEARCH?

Carrying out an effective literature review is an important skill for the researcher. It helps to place your work in the context of what has already been done, allowing comparisons to be made, and providing a framework for further research. A literature survey gives an indication of the current state of knowledge and theoretical understanding of the problem being investigated. Spending time reading the literature relevant to your research topic may prevent you from repeating previous errors or redoing work that has already been done. It may well provide you with insights into aspects of your topic that might be worthy of detailed exploration. A review is more than a list of what you have read. It should provide:

- the state of current knowledge on the topic; and

- an account of major questions in the areas which are being investigated or which have been commented on.

Here is some useful guidance for you:

- initially you need to make notes under the points that the writers make, rather than make notes for each author, i.e. analyse rather than describe what each author says;

- you may find it useful to have a sheet of paper for each point and then add comments and quotes as you read;

- write on one side only;

- note down whether you have added a full quotation or a paraphrase;

- do not forget to note the page number and the full reference;

- analyse as you read;

- at the writing stage you can arrange the sheets into the order in which you intend to write;

- make sure that you note the title of the book/paper (for journals note the title of the journal, volume number and issue), author and initial, date of publication, place of publication and page reference;

- be systematic;

- be selective; you must resist the temptation to include irrelevant material; and

- resist the temptation to copy from the texts.

In carrying out a literature review, the aim is to *analyse critically* and *make use of the ideas* to establish the theoretical context and framework of your research that should not take place in a vacuum. In the review you should debate the assumptions and adequacy of the viewpoints you have read. You should be able to illustrate the same argument or assertion from various sources and perspectives as well as criticizing and raising questions related to the points in your review. You need to present your review under relevant points that relate to, and cross-reference, all of your source material. You should *not* present the material book by book or article by article or author by author, rather you need to identify points and issues and analyse them critically. It is absolutely vital that you relate your findings to the issues raised in your review. This may be limited in your assignment, but nevertheless it *must* be attempted.

Searching literature sources

Whether you conduct the literature search for your project manually or by computer, it is sensible to prepare a strategy first which will help you focus your thoughts:

- select your topic

- write out a list of possible keywords

- set some limits:
  - scope
  - time period
  - form of material
  - sector

Finding and using resources

When finding and using resources it might be helpful to keep in mind the points made in Table 11.8.

Table 11.8 Finding and using resources

Define the terminology	• Do you have a clear idea of what the terms mean? • Is your topic open to interpretation? • Think of synonyms. • Look terms up in a good dictionary or in *Roget's Thesaurus*. • Draw a diagram to indicate the possible interpretations.
Define the parameters	• Timescale? – work written since when? • Sources? – books, journals, theses. • Geography? – UK or abroad as well?
Consult:	• British National Bibliography (BNB) – books • British Education Index (BEI) – journals • Computer assisted information acquisition.
Sources:	• books; • prior research studies; • journals; • government documents; • practitioner knowledge; • historical knowledge.

Keeping track of information

Make notes on how you might use the work of other researchers to support or refute your arguments.

• computer/word-processor

• index card system

Listing sources referred to

• name(s) of author(s)

• publication date

• title of book, report, dissertation or article

• names of editor(s) and title of edited collection

• title of journal or magazine (if referring to an article)

• page numbers (for journal or magazine article)

• place of publication and publisher (for a book or report)

WHAT IS VALIDATION? WHY IS IT IMPORTANT IN THE CONTEXT OF ACTION RESEARCH?

Making a claim that your research has resulted in improvement, even with supportive evidence, does not automatically make it credible. That credibility will only come from presenting your work to others, seeking their agreement

Table 11.9 Types of validation

Type of validation	Key questions to aid reflection
Self	• How can I demonstrate to my own satisfaction that I have done what I had planned to do? • How can I demonstrate to my own satisfaction that I have carried out a systematic enquiry that has helped me live out my values more successfully than before? • How rational an account could I present of the personal learning that has resulted from this enquiry?
Peer	• How would I be able to convince a group of peers that my claim to improved knowledge should be taken seriously? • How might I convince them that I am demonstrating responsible and exemplary practice? • How clearly would I be able to set out the criteria for assessing my work? • How would I ensure that my evidence around these criteria is unambiguous?
Line management	• In what ways would I show my line managers that I have intervened in my professional practice to improve it? • How would I convince my line managers that my way of working could be adopted to bring about wider benefits?

and making any necessary adjustments. There are several forms of validation, as shown in Table 11.9.

The above list is by no means exhaustive. It does not take account, for example, of action research that may be presented to the academic community as part of higher academic study. Whichever group is relevant to your situation, they need to be sympathetic to what you are trying to do, but capable of giving constructive and critical feedback. Only in this way can the work be evaluated on its own merit.

HOW DO I WRITE UP MY ACTION RESEARCH? IN WHAT FORM SHOULD I PRESENT IT?

Many worry that their research has to be published in academic journals. This is certainly not the case; it could, however, constitute a valuable professional development opportunity at some stage. The key consideration is how the outcomes of your research may be made accessible to a wider public. This means knowing your audience and deciding upon an appropriate format for doing so. It is not the intention here to provide a full description of alternative methods of reporting. However, in this section the focus is on communicating the meaning of your research in the form of a written report. Whatever you write, it should reflect not only yourself, and your particular style, but also the nature and context of the research question. Remember that you are telling a story – one that you can organize chronologically, by themes, by data source, or any other way – it is up to you! Generally speaking, there are five structural elements for an action research report. Although these elements are described in a particular order, they need not be that way in your report. In fact, they do not even need to be separated from one another.

1. The context

The first element of the action research report is a description of the context within which the action research took place. Depending on the project that you do, the locus of the context can be your classroom, your school, or your area of responsibility, e.g. pastoral head, subject coordinator, examinations secretary. It is possible that the context of the project includes aspects of more than one of these. It is important to remember that the physical description of the setting is important, but that there are other aspects that are important depending on the project. For example, if your project focuses on working with parents or students, a description of these populations should be included.

2. Statement and origin of your research focus

The statement of your research focus should answer one or more of the following questions:

- What did I investigate?
- What have I accomplished or attempted to accomplish in this study?
- What have been my goals?

This element of the report should also address the way in which your starting point developed. That is:

- How did the idea originate?
- How and why did it change through the year?
- What impact did my research notebook group have on the development of my starting point?

In addition, this section should include what you learned from reading the research literature that informed your study.

3. Methods

This element of the report focuses on the way in which you investigated your practice situation. Your task, in the report, is to respond to the following kinds of questions:

- What did I do and why?
- What sort of data did I collect?
- How did I collect the data?

- What successes or difficulties did I have in carrying out this action research?

4. The findings

The fourth element of the report states what it was that you accomplished and/or found out. Remember that all action research projects involve actions so therefore there are effects of those actions. And every action research project results in the teacher coming to a new understanding of his or her own educational situation. Therefore each report should contain some description of what it was that you learned. Make sure to include any events, circumstances or data that contradict what you had hoped to do or find out.

5. Implications

Although this element is labelled *implications*, it is not necessary that each project has far-reaching effects. These implications could be a statement of how participation in this research has affected the ways in which you look at your teaching, your pupils, or your team/school. In other words, do you see the educational world differently now, and how will that affect what it is that you will do next?

6. The next step

Finally, include a paragraph describing the next step of this research. Is it complete? Is there another scenario you wish to research? Explain how you would continue action research, following up on this study or developing a new idea.

Overall, this structure is not dissimilar to what you may be familiar with – the standard research report. There is a general introduction that places the research within the field, a statement of the problem or hypothesis, the method used, findings of the research, and finally, implications. But it can be significantly different because you may feel free to write in the first person and to use a narrative style – to tell a validated story. You may find the overall structure shown in Table 11.10 of some help when structuring your report:

SUMMARY SELF-REVIEW

Spend a little time considering and then responding to the following review questions:

1. How have I improved my professional practice?

2. In what ways have I improved my understanding of this practice so that it is more just?

3. How have I used my knowledge and influence to improve the situation – at team, school and community levels?

Table 11.10 Possible structure for your final report

Part of report	What each part should contain
Title	Include the title of your study, your name and the date. The title should accurately reflect the nature of your study and should be brief and to the point. A subtitle may be provided if it clarifies the purpose of the study.
Acknowledgements	You may wish to acknowledge the help given to you in conducting your research. If so, acknowledgements and thanks generally come after the title page.
Contents	This section should list the contents of your report and appropriate page referencing and should assist readers to find their way around the project.
Abstract	Here, you are expected to say in a few words what your research project sets out to do, the methods employed and what conclusions have been reached.
Introduction	An introduction should 'set the scene'. It needs briefly to place the research issue in context and indicate why the issue is worthy of research.
Literature review	A literature survey should indicate the current state of knowledge and theoretical understanding of the issue.
Research questions/aims/ hypotheses	Include any research questions and your reasons for posing them. These should be related to the literature survey and the approaches to data collection and analysis.
Methodology	The methodology needs to be explained and justified in terms of suitability and operationalization.
Data collecting methods	Specific data collecting techniques should be discussed and justified with issues of reliability and validity dealt with.
Data analysis methods	The analysis of all data is presented in this section. Data should be presented for easy use and reference by the reader.
Discussion/conclusions	The discussion deals with both the extent to which any research questions have been answered by the research and how it contributes to relevant practice and theory.
Reflection	Shortcomings of the research are best presented here, as are recommendations for further work and action in the light of the research.
References	This section provides details of the sources referred to in the text. Make sure that you follow appropriate formats, e.g. the Harvard author-date system.
Bibliography	This section provides details of all other sources consulted.
Appendices	This is where all your raw data is presented.

4. In what ways have I taken responsibility for my own action?

5. How have I learned from my own practice and made changes where necessary?

6. What evidence is there that I have incorporated into my explanation others' perspectives on the action?

7. How have I involved others in setting the agenda of the research and in interpreting the outcomes?

8. In what ways have I shared ownership of the action research with others?

9. How effectively have I explained my own educational practice in terms of an evaluation of past practice and an intention to create an improvement which is not yet in existence?

10. How have I described and explained my learning and educational development that is part of the process of answering the research question?

11. How have I integrated my values with the theories of others as explanatory principles?

12. How effectively have I monitored what was happening?

13. What evidence have I found to support my claims about action?

14. How secure are the professional judgements that will inform subsequent action?

15. How rigorously have I tested the strength of my evidence and the validity of my judgements with other teachers and academic peers?

16. In what ways have I influenced the situation?

Action planning

Having spent some time reviewing your approach to creating a culture of action research within your team, identify some actions that you might take to strengthen your current approach.

Bibliography

Armstrong, M. (1988) *A Handbook of Personnel Management Practice* (2nd edition). London: Kogan Page.

Armstrong, M. (1994) *How To Be an Even Better Manager*. London: Kogan Page.

Bassey, M. (1998) Action Research for Improving Education Practice. In R. Halsall (ed.), *Teacher Research and School Improvement: Opening doors from the inside*. Buckingham: Open University Press.

Belbin, R.M. (1981) *Management Teams: Why They Succeed or Fail*. Oxford: Heinemann.

Bell, L. (1992) *Managing Teams in Secondary Schools*. London: Routledge.

Bennis, W. (1989) *On Becoming a Leader*. London: Hutchinson.

Bennis, W. and Nanus, B. (1985) *Leaders: The Strategies for Taking Charge*. New York: Harper & Row.

Blake, R. and Mouton, J. (1964) *The Managerial Grid*. Houston, Texas: Gulf.

Blaxter, L., Hughes, C. and Tight, M. (1996) *How To Research*. Buckingham: Open University Press.

Bolton, R. (1987) *People Skills*. Sydney: Simon and Schuster.

Boydell, T. (1985) *Management Self-Development: A Guide for Managers, Organisations and Institutions*. Geneva: International Labour Organisation.

Bryant, I. (1996) Action Research and Reflective Practice. In D. Scott and R. Usher (eds) *Understanding Educational Research*. London: Routledge.

Bryman, A. (1986) *Leadership and Organizations*. London: Routledge & Kegan Paul.

Bush, T. and Middlewood, D. (eds) (1997) *Managing People in Education*. London: Paul Chapman Publishing.

Covey, S. (1989) *The Seven Habits of Effective People*. London: Simon and Schuster.

Covey, S. (1992) *Principle-Centred Leadership*. London: Simon and Schuster.

Day, C., Hall, C. and Whitaker, P. (1998) *Developing Leadership in Primary Schools*. London: Paul Chapman Publishing.

Dean, J. (2002) *Implementing Performance Management: A handbook for schools*. London: Routledge Falmer.

DfEE (2000) *Performance Management in Schools: Performance Management Framework* (DfEE 0051/2000). London: The Stationery Office.

DfES (2001a) *The Teachers' Standards Framework* (DfES 0647/2001). London: The Stationery Office.

DfES (2001b) *The Education (School Teacher Appraisal) (England) Regulations*. Statutory Instrument 2001, No. 2855. London: The Stationery Office.

Downey, M. (2001) *Effective Coaching*. New York: Texere Publishing.

Drucker, P. (1988) *Management*. London: Pan Books.

Elliott, J. (1991) *Action Research for Educational Change*. Milton Keynes: Open Unversity Press.

Everard, R.D. (1998) *Coaching and the Art of Management*. London: Coaching Connection.

Everard, B. and Morris, G. (1996) *Effective School Management* (3rd edition). London: Paul Chapman Publishing.

Fox, A. (2002) *Managing Conflict*. London: Spiro Press.

Glatthorn, A.A. (1990) *Supervisory Leadership*. Glenview, IL: Scott, Foresman/ Little, Brown Higher Education.

Goleman, D. (1996) *Emotional Intelligence*. London: Bloomsbury.

Goodworth, C.T. (1985) *Effective Delegation*. London: Business Books.

Gunter, H. (2001) *Leaders and Leadership in Education*. London: Paul Chapman Publishing.

Hall, V. and Oldroyd, D. (1990) *Management Self-Development for Staff in Secondary Schools, Unit 2: Policy, Planning and Change*. Bristol: NDCEMP.

Hall, V., Wallace, M. and Hill, T. (1991) *Management Self-Development, Module 2, Book 2*. Bristol: NDCEMP.

Handy, C.B. (1993) *Understanding Organisations* (4th edition). Harmondsworth: Penguin.

Heemsbergen, B. (2000) 'Coaching from the inside out: Creating exceptional results'. *Leadership Compass Banff Centre* (Summer/Fall), 3, 7–9.

Hersey, P. and Blanchard, K. (1977) *Management of Organizational Behaviour: Utilizing Human Resources*. London: Prentice Hall International.

Herzberg, F., Mausner, B. and Snyderman, B.B. (1959). *The Motivation to Work* (2nd edition). New York: John Wiley & Sons.

Hodgson, P. (1987) 'Managers can be taught, but leaders have to learn'. *ICT*, November/December, 14–23.

Honey, P. and Mumford, A. (1988) *Manual of Learning Styles*. Maidenhead: Peter Honey.

Johnson, D. (1994) *Research Methods in Educational Management*. London: Longman.

Jones, J.L. (2001) *Performance Management for School Improvement*. London: Fulton.

Kemmis, S. (1988) Action Research. In J.P. Keeves (ed.) *Education Research, Methodology and Measurement: An International Handbook*. London: Pergamon Press, pp. 42–9.

Kemmis, S. and McTaggart, R. (1982) *The Action Research Planner*. Victoria: Deakin University Press.

Kerr, S. (ed.) (1998) *Ultimate Rewards: What Really Motivates People to Achieve*. Cambridge, MA: Harvard Business School Press.

Kolb, D.A. (1984) *Experiential Learning: Experience as the Source of Learning and Development*. Englewood Cliffs, NJ: Prentice-Hall.

Kouzes, J.M. and Posner, B.Z. (1993) *The Leadership Challenge*. San Francisco: Jossey Bass Wiley.

Law, S. and Glover, D. (2000) *Educational Leadership and Learning*. Buckingham: Open University Press.

Leithwood, K., Jantzi, D. and Steinbach, R. (1999) *Changing Leadership for Changing Times*. Buckingham: Open University Press.

Lessem, R. (1991) *Total Quality Learning*. Oxford: Blackwell.

Lewin, K. (1951) *Field Theory in Social Science*. New York: Harper & Row.

Lewis, I. and Munn, P. (1987) *So You Want To Do Research*. Edinburgh: SCRE.

Lomax, P. (2002) Action Research. In M. Coleman and A. Briggs (eds) *Research Methods in Educational Leadership and Management*. London: Paul Chapman Publishing.

Louis, K.S. and Miles, M.B. (1992) *Improving the Urban High School: What Works and Why*. London: Cassell.

Maslow, A.H. (1943) 'A Theory of Human Motivation'. *Psychological Review*, 50. 370–96.

MacBeath, J. and Myers, K. (1999) *Effective School Leaders: How to evaluate and Improve Your Leadership Potential*. London: Pearson.

McGregor, D. (1960) *The Human Side of Enterprise*. London: McGraw-Hill.

McLeod, D. (2000) *The Coaching and Mentoring Network News* (1 July).

McNiff, J., Lomax, P. and Whitehead, J. (1996) *You and Your Action Research Project*. London: Routledge.

Megginson, D. and Boydell, T. (1979) *A Manager's Guide to Coaching*. London: BACIE.

Naisby, A. (2002) *Appraisal and Performance Management*. London: Spiro Press.

Parkinson, C.N. (1958) *Parkinson's Law*. London: John Murray.

Pedler, M., Burgoyne, J. and Boydell, T. (1986) *Manager's Guide to Self-Development*. Maidenhead: McGraw-Hill Education.

Peters, T. and Austin, N. (1986) *A Passion for Excellence*. London: Fontana.

Rowe, D. (1989) *The Successful Self: Freeing Our Hidden Inner Strengths*. New York: Harper Collins.

Schein, E. (1985) *Organizational Culture and Leadership*. San Francisco: Jossey-Bass.

Senge, P.M., Kleiner, A., Roberts, C., Ross, R.B. and Smith, B.J. (1996) *The Fifth Discipline Fieldbook*. London: Nicholas Brealey.

Tannenbaum, R. and Schmidt, W. (1959) 'How to choose a leadership pattern'. *Harvard Business Review*, 51(3), 162–80.

Thomas, K. (1976) Conflict and Conflict Management. In Marvin D. Dunnette (ed.) *Handbook of Industrial and Organisational Psychology*. Chicago: Rand McNally.

Tuckman, B.W. (1965) Development sequences in small groups. *Psychological Bulletin*, 63(1), 53–64.

Warwick, D. (1983) *Decision Making*. London: The Industrial Society.

White, R. and Lippitt, R. (1983) Leadership behaviour and member reactions in three social climates In C. Cartwright and A. Zander (eds) *Group Dynamics*. London: Tavistock Publishing.

Woodcock, M. (1979) *Team Development Manual*. Aldershot: Gower.

Zaleznik, A. (1977) 'Managers and leaders: are they different?' *Harvard Business Review*, 55(3), 67–78.

Index